The UNDERGROUND CHURCH

THE UNDERGROUND CHURCH

Edited by MALCOLM BOYD

SHEED AND WARD : New York

© *Sheed and Ward, Inc., 1968*

Library of Congress Catalog Card Number 68-17361

Manufactured in the United States of America

Contents

PREFACE *by Malcolm Boyd*   *vii*

CONTRIBUTORS   *ix*

1/ *Ecclesia Christi*   *3*
     by Malcolm Boyd

2/ The People of the Underground Church   *7*
     by Layton P. Zimmer

3/ Toward a United Peace and Freedom Church   *31*
     by John Pairman Brown

4/ Diary from the Underground   *50*
     by Daniel Berrigan, S.J.

5/ Litany from the Underground, I   *63*
     by Robert W. Castle, Jr.

6/ The Church and Civil Rights   *70*
     by James E. Groppi

7/ Black Power vis-à-vis "The Kingdom of God"   *84*
     by James E. P. Woodruff

8/ Church as Counter-sign: Process and Promise   *102*
     by Michael F. Groden and
     Sister Miriam Clasby, S.N.D. de Namur

9/ A Baptism Rite   *115*
   by Andy McGowan

10/ Up from the Underground   *120*
   by George J. Hafner

11/ Emmaus: A Venture in Community and
   Communication   *138*
   by David Kirk

12/ Litany from the Underground, II   *152*
   by Robert W. Castle, Jr.

13/ The Missionary and the Black Man   *159*
   by Speed B. Leas

14/ The Church: Served or Serving   *177*
   by Naomi L. M. Long

15/ The World, My Church; My Life, My Prayer   *193*
   by Sharon Murdoch

16/ The Invisible Christian   *207*
   by Robert E. Grossmann

17/ A Bishop Views the Underground Church   *221*
   by the Rt. Rev. Paul Moore, Jr.

18/ *Imitatio Christi*   *238*
   by Malcolm Boyd

Preface

Not in any sense a formal collection of academic treatises, this book is rather a combination of exploratory and highly individual statements reflecting participation in a Christian movement which is frequently called the Underground Church. There is considerable divergence as well as unity evidenced in the individual statements. They are not so much *about* the movement as simply voices speaking *from* within it. The personalities—and the concerns, views, experiences, and hopes—of the writers stand out sharply, contributing to diversity in the work as well as spontaneity and underlying solidarity.

M. B.

Contributors

DANIEL BERRIGAN, S.J., is presently on the faculty of Cornell University. He has published eight books, four of them collections of his poetry.

MALCOLM BOYD is ecumenical chaplain-at-large to American university students and author of *Are You Running with Me, Jesus?*

JOHN PAIRMAN BROWN is Professor of Christian Ethics and New Testament at the Church Divinity School of the Pacific in Berkeley, California.

ROBERT W. CASTLE, JR., is stationed at St. John's Church, a core-city parish in Jersey City, New Jersey.

MIRIAM CLASBY, S.N.D. DE NAMUR, is coordinator of the Hawthorne House Urban Education Center in Roxbury, Massachusetts. She is also the chairman of the Sisters' Committee of the Boston Catholic Interracial Council.

MICHAEL F. GRODEN is director of Saint Joseph Housing, Inc., in Roxbury, Massachusetts, and was one of the initial planners of Hawthorne House.

JAMES E. GROPPI is adviser to the Milwaukee N.A.A.C.P. Youth Council and the leader of demonstrations for open housing in that city. He has recently received an award from the N.A.A.C.P. for his contributions to civil rights.

ROBERT E. GROSSMANN has been president of the National Federation of Catholic College Students for two terms.

GEORGE J. HAFNER is chaplain to the Christian Laymen's Experimental Organization, an "ecumenical" parish in the Trenton, New Jersey, area.

DAVID KIRK, a native of Alabama, is the founder and coordinator of Emmaus House, an ecumenical community dedicated to an experimental ministry in East Harlem, New York City.

SPEED B. LEAS is director of COMMIT, the Center of Metropolitan Mission In-service Training in Los Angeles, California.

NAOMI L. M. LONG has administered metropolitan church youth programs and has worked with the rural poor in Mississippi.

ANDY MCGOWAN conducts the "Talk Back" program on WBAI-FM in New York City.

PAUL MOORE, JR., is the Suffragan Episcopal Bishop of Washington, D. C., and author of *The Church Reclaims the City.*

SHARON MURDOCH, a senior at Radford College in Virginia, spent two summers working with underprivileged preschool children in an ecumenical project.

JAMES E. P. WOODRUFF served as chaplain to Fisk University, Tennessee Agricultural and Industrial College, and Meharry Medical College. He is now the Associate Director of the Department of Communications of the Episcopal Diocese of Pennsylvania.

LAYTON P. ZIMMER edited *The Church and Riots* and is now Deputy Director of the Peace Corps in the Fiji Islands.

The UNDERGROUND CHURCH

1 / *Ecclesia Christi*

by MALCOLM BOYD

The Ecumenical movement and the dynamism of John XXIII and Vatican II provided the impetus for the Underground Church; it would clearly not have emerged as a movement at this time in history without them.

Yet each aroused expectations which could not pragmatically be satisfied hierarchically as *noblesse-oblige* handouts; so a double thrust of reaction to debilitating organizational slowness followed initial action, set in motion by ecumenical activity and response to a worldwide cry for the discovery of human meaning amid threats of dehumanization and even annihilation.

The Underground Church never set out to "replace" the Establishment Church, let alone to "become" it. The Underground Church must, in a real sense, be seen as a radical and contemporary extension of what, for lack of a better word, may be called Christian renewal. This is a strand in Church history which discernibly may be found again and again—a Bernard of Clairvaux here, a Catherine of Sienna there; a Francis, a Luther, a Wesley—the list is a continuing one, for history is being made as well as studied. More recently, one might wish to discuss the inclusion of Dietrich Bonhoeffer or Simone Weil or Henri Perrin.

"Renewal" has often seemed to be misinterpreted, perhaps deliberately, to render a false appearance of "liberalism" as

3

a means of avoiding downright radical change. One seldom hears this word in the movement of the Underground Church. The concept it incarnates has, to a considerable degree, been bypassed; one is now talking about structural change instead of superficial rearrangement. It is no longer a matter of deciding whether or not to sweep dirt underneath a rug, for many of the rugs have been taken up.

There must undeniably be impasse after impasse in the complex, ambiguous relations between the hard-to-locate Underground Church and the Establishment Church with an address, telephone number, and bank account. An older officialdom, accustomed to obedience, must experience shock after shock as traditional obedience is simply denied, not angrily, but because there is now a new (new?, no!, rediscovered) yoke to be worn. So obedience continues to be basic, but its source is different. The Underground is often saying, let the Church *be itself*—*not* denominational ghettos with historical excuses, *not* private clubs with local membership qualifications based on race or economics, *not* costumed dispensers of would-be (and often advertised) "magic," *not* playing games with "God" for an hour a week, *not* a labyrinth of man-made legalisms, *not* an organizational structure which must remain unquestioned and, therefore, unchanged—but *itself,* which means a community of servanthood in the midst of the world's concerns. This community resists the incestuousness of "religion" as an idolatry, and it seeks honestly to find what it means to be the Body of Christ *now, here,* with *this* person, in *this* situation, in *this* moment.

To be silent: so often the Establishment Church has succumbed to this pressure of imagined neutrality. Cathedrals were completed, schools and parish halls built, salaries miraculously provided for liberal experimental ministries—and the Church remained the chaplain of the status quo. Price tags on all the gargoyles! A young, outspoken, idealistic cleric was silenced or quietly moved—this, accomplished usually without sweat or public scandal, "decently and in order."

The Underground is aware that Christianity is not only a movement but is institutionalized. However, institution can easily move into a mined field of self-serving organization and stifling authoritarianism. By its very nature, the Underground *must* experiment with new ideas and forms. This is threatening to the Establishment. The action of the Eucharist must be demonstrated in style, color, movement, and music; the Underground will not wait for official commissions to take five or ten years for discussion, and, even then, perhaps come up with anachronistically irrelevant guidelines. Yet the Underground's main task is to look *outside* Church structure, to see the people in the world and love them.

One finds in the Underground a breakdown of old dichotomies. There are homegrown liturgies in city after city; men, Catholic and Protestant, are writing baptism services for their own children; couples are composing marriage services, these to be held in home settings: yet the Underground is *not* withdrawing from the world, but embracing it. Theology itself is understood as a vital relating of faith and life in concrete action; religious questions are seen to concern poverty, war, and race, rather than "the Virgin Birth" or the composition of the Trinity. Underground clergy are turning to secular employment which brings them very, very close to people in an unstagey, natural work- and life-environment.

The Underground Church is sensitively aware of simplistic, naive entrapments: self-righteousness, a self-made identification with "the remnant," the supposed destruction of institution (as one structure is torn down, another is going up), social gospel, pure community versus corrupt perversion of community, and so on.

The present Underground Church is a movement which has two basic drives which are identical with those of the Ecumenical movement: Church unity and radical involvement of the Church in the social concerns of contemporary life. In its actions, the Underground Church, in connection with both of these drives, has acted far more radically than has the Establishment Church. It has practiced Church unity across forbidden eucharistic lines, experimenting liturgically with the meaning, for men and women living today, of "worship." And it has been free of the pressures brought to bear by the social Establishment upon the Establishment Church. So it has become closely identified, in various sectors and ways, with so-called secular humanists in movements related to race, peace, and poverty. In fact, "the Church" has been "found" in many so-called secular movements within society, and yet at the same time seems not to be present in many of the programs and activities of the Establishment Church. *Involvement* and *commitment,* in the sense of presence within the secular arena and outside "churchianity," have become key concepts in the Underground Church.

2/ The People of
the Underground Church

by LAYTON P. ZIMMER

Bright, early morning sun streams through ground mist and
living-room windows, touching the heads of the standing
group with soft light. A White businessman reads the Epistle;
a Black housewife reads the Gospel; the group is silent for a
moment and then, quite slowly and softly, someone begins the
Creed. A Lutheran minister in shirt and tie, assisted by an
Episcopal worker-priest in bermudas and sport shirt, celebrates the Eucharist by an experimental Anglican rite; and the
two administer the sacrament to one Roman Catholic clergyman and several Roman Catholic laity, a Presbyterian minister, two Methodist laymen, two Black Power agnostics, a Uni-
versalist hippie from Harvard, an elderly birthright Quaker
lady and a French Reform Church nun from Switzerland. The
three Jews present join in prayers as their personal theologies
permit and refuse communion, but kneel (one stands)
throughout. Then, a hurried meal shared from what each has
been able to bring with him: pastries, orange juice, cold bacon
for those who can face it, and lots of thermos coffee, with or
without. There is no beginning of an agenda; just conversation
slowly centering down on one or two immediate, common
concerns, naturally evolving into a circle of talk: problems
presented; reactions and answers explored; hatreds con-

7

fronted; humor enjoyed. Then, one or two must get to work, or go back home to feed the kids lunch; and the group dwindles down and disappears, dispersed.

That's what the Underground Church is! People! Concerned clergy and laity, from all across the whole spectrum of belief and doubt, gathered simply, informally, to share and to gird up each other to work and witness in daily life. Nothing great, or even very impressive! Just people who care about helping each other in a new context, bridging customary separations.

The above is a composite of many such real moments of which I have been a part: most in the Philadelphia area; some in Mobile, New Orleans, Jackson, Sewanee, Hattiesburg, Selma, Detroit, Chester, and in the county garage used as a jail in Media, Pennsylvania.

But Philadelphia is my home and the focus of my concern.

There is still comfort in the traditional, accepted Churches of Philadelphia . . . comfort in the sense of well-appointed seclusion and comfort in the sense of solace. Business, apparently, is as usual, religiously speaking.

Underneath the outward calm, however, one who looks and listens carefully sees worry and shrinking confidence; hears vengeance and desperation. "Anyone who offends so many people the way [that priest] does must be sick. We'll switch him to another mission and get him to a good psychiatrist." "Our financial reports look good but, increasingly, we have to cash in investments to support our present commitments. Lord knows what we'll do to finance our expanded proposals for the future." "Let's put it off! Everybody seems to be so upset right now."

Most faithful followers do not realize what is actually happening to their own denominations. Comfort covers disgust; revolt is there, though mired in centuries' old ruts; hoary endowments are still stretched to subsidize commitment to more relevant secularisms! . . . This is where the Church is today; at least, in Philadelphia.

It is not just that a symbolic sanctifying of civil rights has alienated some of the old folks, although one hears a great deal about this in Church circles. The problem is that so many of the really vital people recognize the emptiness of this and other claims of the Churches to immediacy and meaningfulness. And these are the crucial people who are no longer with the religious scene—not so much driven out (although that is literally true of some), as simply disengaged.

As the institutional Church becomes more self-protective and dishonest, more and more people leave it, or, more accurately, fade away. Relatively few transfer from one branch of rewarding faith to another more lucrative one. Most lapse into quiet nonattendance; some cultivate articulate agnosticism (choices seem to depend largely upon the apparent needs of their children); some continue their search and become participants in the Underground Church.

It's a search for exactly the kind of thing the Churches have been talking about all this time: for explanations; for motivations; for eternal, personal, *real* means and ends in this life. It involves a real rejection (not necessarily consciously decisive, but real nonetheless) of what one has come to realize is mystical hokum. But even that doesn't say it all because every one of us religious types has always lived with at least a sneaking suspicion that the religionness of which we have been such a vital part was somewhat a spoof, a well-intentioned charade. The thing is that now, in our lifetime, the mortally desperate demands of the world reveal the Church as sadly defensive, self-seeking, and ineffectual. The Church, both as an organization and in terms of the persons it vests with holy mystery and sets upon pedestals, is shown by contemporary adversity to be a pious fraud. There are still many who just plain like the feeling of it all—no matter what it might really mean or not mean—so they stick with it; and there are those who are honestly fooled by its appearance of solidity in an unstable time; and there are those who not only get their kicks out of religiousness but can use it for themselves (pay, power, prestige, glory fantasies) and who will hold on as long as they get what they want out of it. But the number sticking is shrinking year by year, and so is the operating total of their money pledges.

It isn't strange that the clergy themselves reflect this unease *and* the searching that it engenders, internally and externally. They are closer than most to the clear apostasy of a meaningless, corrupt Church set in a world of need, yet hopelessly preoccupied with its own wants and illusions. The clergy live and work within sight, so to speak, of the payoff between the power structure of our society and the Churches that structure buys and sells. And, by and large, the clergy are not dumb. Frail, certainly! Wicked, sometimes! Naive, often! Frightened, most of the time! But simply stupid, very rarely. The clergy *do* know what's going on, and they are uncomfortable en masse.

"The Church is institution: a solid, human expression of what we think God wants for our good. People like us—clergy —live by it and for it and from it; and to do this we must live within it. We have made the decision: this diocese cannot emphasize 'mission'; we must be primarily concerned with the maintenance of the institution."

A priest of the Christian Church said this; an ecclesiastical hierarch. In private, of course! These things are not spoken out except in reassurance to a significant contributor or in reprimand of a rebel. Another higher-up, less philosophical, put it more bluntly: "There will be neither preferment within nor recommendation without this diocese for any priest who does not accept the judgment of his superiors in matters of conscience."

No wonder there is a malaise abroad among the clergy. The prophetic voice is interfering with profitable income. The institution of the Church is threatened today—financially, physically—as it has not been for ages.

Those to whom the institution itself is the only meaning of Church in their life are simply falling back on whatever power they can find or manufacture to maintain their prerogatives. Those to whom the structure is as nothing compared to the gospel it has brought to us or to the human needs which call to that gospel are in revolt.

For instance, if you have an idea, an ideal, about the love of God for all men—particularly if you see this through Christ —and you are beginning to get an inkling of the human realities of what man actually does to man, you just cannot live with statements such as this: "It isn't right or wrong that matter, but how you handle the two for the good of the Church." That, too, was said by an important religious official.

The so-called Underground Church grows out of the reaction of human-oriented, gospel idealists to just such statements and the milieu they create. Sensitive people, responsible servants of God, will not affirm such statements, much less worship a god who is claimed to justify them. Even those who seem to buy them without cavil often reveal at least theological insecurity in their aggressive hostility toward those who do question and grow restive.

It is easy to say that the Underground Church is one last refuge for emotional malcontents. It is inexpensive to declare it the deserved end of impractical militants swinging on a Kazantzakis-Pasolini Jesus. Minorities can always be insulted, their members maligned. The members of this minority, however, have lived with accusations and calumny for a long time. Particularly in regard to those charges repeated above, we would tend to agree. Certainly, we are in emotional turmoil, and we have not been "at home" or even sustained heretofore; just as certainly, the Jesus of Graham, Corson, Hines, and Spellman is not apparent to us in the canon of the New Testament *or* in the god-honest works of Kazantzakis and Pasolini. The Underground Church grows precisely because so many feel that Establishment religiousness has failed them and all men more gravely than ever before. Sarcasm and punitive hostility will not heal the breach.

In Philadelphia, the Underground Church is an impetus to prayer and a supplier of bodies for witness, not only when the official Church is not "there," but when it is openly opposed to anyone's being "there." Roman Catholics, Presbyterians, Quakers, Baptists, Lutherans, Unitarians, Methodists, Jews . . . some of all of these, and more, are finding each other walking toward, not talking about, an effective unity based on ministry and witness. All together, they certainly form as diverse a group as you could imagine. Bound together by human experience and understanding, these widely diverse people still try to attend their respective Sabbath services of formal worship. In spite of this, or because of it, they find themselves less and less touched by the stereotyped formalities and more and more in need of the experience-focused sharing of reflection, dialog, and worship that has become the outstanding characteristic of the Underground Church.

For some, it certainly was "civil rights" that started them out on this path of seeking and testing beyond where they'd ever been before. Others began their odyssey in the anguish of personal anonymity suddenly perceived through pastoral platitudes; some in anger at their own and others' apathy; still others in revulsion toward the profits of a politicians' war and national racism.

There seems to be so much less room for myth and fantasy than there was earlier in the lives of most of us. For the concerned citizen today there is no point in arguing whether police brutality, or political corruption, or napalm, or the Birch-Klan axis are real. He is fully able to accept the fact that these aspects of our lives exist.

But, what do *you* think about them? What do *you* want for yourself and others? What will *you* do about your goals? What will *you* give yourself to, and why? These are the questions that make all the difference today.

Some defend the killing of small children in our riot-torn cities as a necessary and inevitable result of a superior's reaction to an inferior's malicious wilfulness. Some are able to support the destruction of a people whose country our leaders claim we must defend to exemplify our own goodness in contrast to the badness we suspect all around us. These people talk a great deal about principles and about their willingness to sacrifice any number of other people (or their sons) in support of the same. These are they who, as some Establishment parishes still do, join in the gathering of pansies in the Spring to pot and take in to place in the window boxes of ghetto tenements.

A metropolitan Philadelphia experiment receives every year thousands of dollars contributed by local and national Church groups with heavy investments in the Philadelphia scene. Two years ago, some of the "hotheads" on the staff of the experiment became involved in overt witness against a racially-segregated public charity. After much discussion, however, the group could only find this lowest-common-denominator consensus: individuals will be allowed freedom of expression, but the name of this group will not be used in support of social causes so that "we will not lose that impartiality that commends us to both sides of every issue." Now, there's a trenchant understanding of the gospel of Jesus Christ, crucified, for you.

The police of the City of Brotherly Love are noted for their personal, physical brutality toward Negroes. General police brutality has resulted in eyes having been beaten or stomped out of the heads of at least three Black men: a father out walking with his children argued with police arresting a sodden drunk ("Don't arrest him. He hasn't done anything. I know him. I'll get him home."); on Christmas Eve, an Army veteran in uniform argued with a Trailways agent about his baggage ticket; a fourteen-year-old boy, loitering, cursed a policeman who had just called him "nigger." Permanent, crippling disfigurement is no part of the law's allowed response to such minor offenses. But, when it happened in Philadelphia, the Churches were silent.

Major religious organizations have been unable to take public stands in support of the American Jewish Committee's invitation to them to join in refusing to hold official meetings in segregated clubs about the city. As one Church official said, "Even though we may not be telling our people directly to quit the clubs, some would feel guilty and we would run the risk of alienating them. Then, what would we do?"

What is the right term to use? Immorality? Amorality? Hypocrisy? Would you believe just "compromise?" Compromise for the sake of survival *now* at any cost . . . this is what is happening. The Church is struggling, sacrificing even its own integrity, to sustain its organic life recognized in terms of buildings, stained glass, real estate, and homiletical whoredom.

Thank God, there are those who see the bankruptcy of such an investment and, trying to avoid cynicism, seek the truth of the way to life in other contexts. They will not gloss over the brutal realities so sanctimoniously accepted by so many churchgoers. Rather, they will declare their loving convictions, asking others to determine for themselves the relationship of dehumanizing commitments to our Judeo-Christian heritage. They are willing to grapple with religious and humanitarian blasphemies so long as they are free to identify them for what they are and combat them openly. And it is right here, at this point, that the communities accepted "aboveground" reject and condemn nonconformists, forcing them into the Underground Church.

Impetus is added by the growing—and justified—Black anger against White liberals. Many spokesmen for disenfranchised, disenchanted Black people have come to understand that racism in America is all-pervasive. They have at last seen the basic truths in the still-continued repression and humiliation of themselves by White people: truths of racial bigotry, class separation, political irresponsibility to constituent citizens, and the immorality of our social apathy. In short, such Black anger has its documentable rationale . . . and it wants no truck with any member (not just with the representatives) of that power structure which preserves, if not actually nourishes, such horrors. So it is that the militant White revolutionary is rejected by the very people who have guided him to question ineffective and dishonest Churches. Having been cut off from the parochial source of much of his idealism, the radical White liberal is also rejected by those with whom he honestly, if not always realistically, wants communion. He may lose himself in frustration or bitterness . . . or he may find the Underground Church.

Some months ago, now, I was asked to leave a Black Power meeting because I am white. Shortly after that, I and other radical clergy and laity were asked to leave a national Church meeting so that those who still believed in the Establishment Church might "talk constructively together." Then, one week after all this, my family and I visited a famous church and heard the promising young pastor deliver a sermon to his wealthy, elderly congregation that can only be summed up as saying: "What lies ahead in eternity is the greatest question—Heaven or Hell!" And more nice people were deluded into thinking that slums, poverty, decay in high places, and churchly silence were unimportant to their own imminent demise and the allocations of their wills.

It is a bad scene! The whole thing is so ridiculous, so empty, so bad. Old-line activists are long gone now, either in dismayed resignation or disgusted escape. Newer liberals don't quite understand; but they sense that much, so much, is missing. And the clergy! Perhaps their lot is the most tragic of all. For, as the specializations of life have developed in these progressive United States, the layman's involvement in and pledge to his parish church has become correspondingly more limited . . . after all, so much of his life lies elsewhere. This process has made it increasingly clear to the clergy that their vocational meaning and value is nil except for the warm pleasures of the Sabbath morning production.

There are many clergy in the Underground Church.

That's an important point; but it's not the only point, nor is it the most significant one. The most important thing is that the Underground Church actually exists. It is made up of clergy and laity, city dwellers and suburbanites, poor and rich, White and Black, churchman and agnostic, old and young. It is an identifiable entity, although it as yet has little general detail. Its members come from all over the place. They're there with a startling array of goals, techniques, hopes, and prayers. With or without membership lists, publicized or not, accidental or thoroughly programmed, the Underground Church is a reality for those who participate in it and, therefore, for those who are touched by the lives of these searching, stumbling people.

The "Alive" group of Roman Catholics now numbers over three hundred members in the Greater Philadelphia area. The group began to form inevitably when the Archbishop (now Cardinal) made clear his intransigent opposition to the civil rights movement of yore, the repair of white-mob-destroyed integrated housing in Folcroft, the reform of police brutality in Chester and Philadelphia, the ecumenical movement, liturgical reform, the Pope's pleas for peace, and change. Priests, surreptitiously active (perhaps already officially disciplined by the Archbishop, but still involved), celebrate Mass for the group and assist in its guidance through discussion and instruction. Laymen, however, remain the basic flesh and spirit of ALIVE.

Years ago, after the attacks on the home of Horace Baker and his family (Negroes who had moved into a lower-class, White suburb) had subsided in Folcroft, and the Chester police were cleaning the blood off their nightsticks, I received a series of anonymous phone calls from Roman Catholic housewives in the area, members of an ad-hoc grouping that later influenced the formation of the Alive group. They said only that they cared desperately about the horror that had happened; that they were ashamed of their Archbishop's apathy in rebuking neither the ferocious mobs of Folcroft nor the brutal police of Chester as well as in not supporting the few who dared to challenge the one-party political corruption of the county of which both communities are a part. Each caller ended by reassuring me that all of us actively involved in the struggle were constantly in their prayers; that we must continue to work and witness, not only for "civil rights," but for the sake of those who had not yet found an overt way to participate. This was my first exposure to what we now call the Underground Church.

Today, unofficial and underground though it is, the Alive group is represented in almost every ecumenical, interracial discussion about social problems. And it is a bravely active group. It has picketed the Cardinal's residence on several occasions, as well as the Chancery office by the downtown great cathedral. More importantly, ALIVE has not only protested racial, social, and religious problems, but its members are beginning to conceive of their role as that of coalescing others outside their communion into a more widely representative group with broader, deeper concerns. In this last, they are increasingly effective, working with and through secular social agencies as well as through their extensive contacts among the clergy and laity of other religious groups.

In 1965, active involvement in Fair Housing became the base for another group. Representing a broad spectrum of the religious community—Jews, Quakers, Baptists, Presbyterians, Unitarians, and others—they began holding small meetings in homes simply to be together in the newfound commonality of their cause and their hurt. There weren't many, all told, but they had deep commitment to social justice, and they were able to find and express their shared need for the support of one another. Starting with prayer, meditation, discursive good fellowship, and planning, this group (which never presumed to name itself or to count its membership) grew to the point of holding retreats outside the city so that together, and often with whole families gathered too, they could enjoy relevant worship and conversation and the healing of sympathetic relationships. They called in speakers and worship leaders from other cities. Above all, they found the strength and direction among themselves to redouble their efforts in the worldly battles of their lives. This group is presently examining its goals and methods, facing more experimentation as it develops both the quality of its internal life and the effectiveness of its members' roles in social change.

There is still another group, but one more highly specialized and limited both in membership and impact. It is a group of Episcopalians, many of them clergy, who meet as little as possible, and when they do, it is primarily to pray and talk together (note how these same objectives are shared in all the separate cells of the Underground Church), to find sustenance spiritually, mentally, and emotionally in order to better understand and fulfill their functions in the ongoing revolution in our land. This group has both name and membership lists. Although it has met only twice in the past half-year, its members have grown close long since in demonstrations, bomb-watches, passing out leaflets, diocesan politicking, crisis meetings, and in the special frustration of Episcopalians (we are known to be such liberals; but we never challenge our own constituency past a certain point, and we have no room for radicals). At the suggestion of an Underground churchman in Washington, D.C., the group calls itself "The Conspiracy for Good." It is made up of exactly twenty-three people: nine laymen and fourteen clergymen.

All of the groups mentioned so far have fairly orthodox—or, at least, variations on the traditional—liturgies. The Alive group still celebrates Mass, following the basic formulas of the Roman Rite, with contemporary, vernacular insertions. The "outgrowth" group follows both anciently-customary and extemporaneous usages, leaving liturgy to the spirit of a particular occasion and to the inspiration of the leader. The Conspiracy group has utilized a generally Episcopal form of eucharistic celebration, always in the context of informality: following the Prayer Book, yet extensively using extemporaneous prayers, with celebrant priests in street clothes. In this sense, too, the Conspiracy group is like the other groups . . . it tends to rely on the accustomed uses of its members for its expression of worship, rather than leaping off into folk, rock, or psychedelic celebrations.

The groups are similar in other ways as well. These notes, recorded at a Conspiracy meeting, might well be fragments of records from the discussions of any cells of the Underground Church:

National interest, personal interest, not religion or any such simplistic ideology make *the* difference to contemporary churchmen.

Structures can be heretical, not just thoughts and words. Structures are based on assumptions that always devolve into irrelevance or heresy through time and change. Christians should be committed to *movement,* not *institutions.* They should be concerned with their presence where it counts, in the world.

Our first job is neither to save nor to destroy the Church, but to be involved in the agenda of the practical realities of life as followers of Christ, lover and brother of all mankind.

Our religious establishment cannot face conflict within itself or between itself and the world. It doesn't look right by the standards we have adopted for self-protection. It isn't just a problem of communication; there *are* some things that are realistically unpleasant and unpopular—war, poverty, racist educational systems, and the suburban rape of the city. No one makes money out of

---

being unpleasant, so the Church is bought and sold. Only *after* commitment and action is reflection and valid personal identification possible . . . and the Church is afraid of commitment and action.

There are two ways to change: friendly persuasion, consensus, mediation [the religious establishment]; and conflict, politics, coercion [the real world]. Why don't we form a conspiracy for good to catalyze useful conflict, supporting each other . . . and restraining each other from using the conflict or its ramifications for personal gain?

O.K. But remember! This is total difference about which we're talking now. And it won't be very acceptable to many others. We can list the differences . . . :

INSTITUTIONAL CHURCH	UNDERGROUND CHURCH
uniting	dividing
openness	covertness
consensus	conflict
trust	suspicion
persuasion	manipulation
flight	fight
generalization	specificity
discussion	action
full communication	selected communication
high visibility	low visibility

It looks like a rough plot of the Gospels compared to a scenario written by Norman Vincent Peale; but Nathan Hale would have bought it.

And so it went. Unlike other unofficial organizations within the body of a formal religious institution, there was no final draft of a charter. The Conspiracy group *evolved* out of thoughts like these, as did the other identifiable "parishes" in the Underground Church.

The mainstay of the Underground Church in Philadelphia is a comparatively visible group called "Wellsprings," which is presently applying for foundation support. Stronger and larger than any of the others, the Wellsprings group is headed by an ex-Quaker, now a Roman Catholic, John Stokes. He has worked closely with a local Methodist Church to raise up a gathering of people pragmatically concerned with God and man. Openly avowing their dedication to making a practical difference in this life, the members of WELLSPRINGS are a true faithful remnant of our time. They are the minorities of the various communions and judicatories willing to face any apathy or opposition as they seek to improve the circumstances of human life for reasons that lie beyond themselves.

Two types of movement are clear within the Wellsprings group. First, the basic in-and-out brings concerned people together for mutual support and shared growth and disperses them again to personally possible action. Second, the Wellsprings group has developed from Methodist sponsorship with ecumenical intentions to a pan-Protestant group and to Protestant-Roman Catholic, to Christian-Jewish, to Black-White, to religious-secular, to war-peace involvements.

Besides confronting sacred and temporal problems of our day, WELLSPRINGS is given to building communication-bridges between polarized people and forces. Likewise, they are concerned to pool their skills of mind, hand, and money in the accomplishment of social change. In some ways, the most important thing this largely middle-class body does is to seek out realities beyond their own experience and record them.

For those who care or who can be led or forced to hear, the Wellsprings group has amassed a detailed, pertinent collection of authentic data of the sin and suffering of our locale. It is not merely evidence; it is an anguished, angry scream that drowns out the pretentious contentions of creeds and makes clear the irrelevance of budgets to morality.

John Stokes has led the Wellsprings people to seek a

way of bringing the Underground Church up above ground into an ecumenical working relationship with the institutional Church and synagogue . . . (1) working through community congregational structures to convene their socially concerned minorities, thus bringing them above ground, and (2) establishing an announced working relationship with denominational bodies which is acknowledgedly experimental, exploratory, radical, risk-taking, controversy-developing,—again bringing our relationship with them above ground."

Stokes and his board envision working out "a consultative and collaborative relationship without implicating them [the religious institutions] in our explorations or relinquishing our own freedom of innovation and integrity. We address ourselves to critical needs and ask only for financial help from the established Churches."

In an organized way, that's all there is to the Underground Church in Philadelphia. Social and political activists who have been trained and nourished within the religious community have found that their sensitive response to need and crisis has far outstripped the wordy, programmatic mediocrity of the denominational response to the travail of the less fortunate of God's children. Not all revolutionaries by a long shot, they have been pushed by realities into criticism, disillusionment, separation, and, finally, into new associations in subterranean power-groupings. It all doesn't mean much yet in the success terms of our national *hubris* . . . but it is there, and it intends to make a great deal of difference in times to come. So, who knows?

Worship in the context of the lives we live; candid conversation; compassionate relationships; strength, guidance, and encouragement for commitment . . . these are the things the Underground Church means to me. To those of us who have found ourselves a part of events and circumstances we never planned, the Underground Church has come to make all the difference in the world; and we can't stop trying to bring about a like change in the lives of others.

Some years ago—about twelve, now, I guess—I remember sitting in on a bull session of other, older clergy right after I had just been priested (after a year's diaconate). They asked me to tell them honestly what I thought of "Sunday mornings." I mustered up my honesty and admitted I was still dismayed by the fact that, for all their moments of ceremonial glory, Sunday mornings were personal hell because of all the facades that had to be assumed (as seminary had taught us to do) in order to be at least something pleasant to everybody—including those who talked about "niggers," sterilizing the poor, and the preventive H-bombing of Russia. There was a pause in the conversation, and I was afraid I had offended my seniors. Then, one older priest smiled in a kind of sad way, and I, covering, asked too loudly what *they* thought of "Sunday mornings." More silence! Then a cough, and one said, "The Church, to me, is small groups of intimate friends getting together, having supper, and just being there a while with each other. At least this is real and it helps us all. Sunday mornings don't, very often, really help anybody, do they?"

Perhaps, in retrospect, we might agree that this priest, this *man,* was a precursor of what we now identify as the Underground Church. Perhaps the clergy gathered that night were a primitive "conspiracy for good." Certainly, they were at home with each other and they shared ups and downs, hopes and disgust, in an easy familiar way.

It is important that the Underground Church is nourishment, focus, and stimulation for the carrying out of one's calling in spite of, or even in opposition to, the guardians of yesterday's safest courtesies. It is important because it is helping people realize their humanity as well as their calling of "Otherness." It helps them find and maintain their freedom to dissent, to criticize, and it shares strength to take the hard steps away from rewarding conformity toward the harsh meanings of challenge and change.

In a way, however, even these relatively amorphous gatherings of mutually concerned people can become dangerous to the best things they seek to find and cultivate. The Established Church has taught us that with even the most rudimentary beginnings of formalization man in his religiosity tends to sanctify his fears, his popularity- and prestige-needs, his power drives, and his exclusivity. Internal stability and mutual regard can become cannibalistic idols in themselves . . . and these Molochs are constructed by well-meaning religionists who think they have found an answer to the mysteries and problems of living faithfully in what they regard as a faithless and profane world.

This scares the daylights out of me. As a student of liturgics, I am far too prone to delight in the rites that have been ceremoniously presented to me by my fathers; I tend not even to notice the sin-chains of exclusivistic "rightness" they put on my relations to God and my fellowman. So, I have to struggle not to preserve customs that immensely satisfy me and not to forcibly attempt to pass them on to those who live in tomorrow's different world. We Anglicans delight in the revolutionary loveliness of the seventeenth century, but it surely hasn't helped us to be redeemingly significant in the twentieth.

It takes money to develop ceremonies; and successful organization demands the profits of compromise. We all know that business and politics are the successful exploitation of the "art of the possible," plus the manipulation of advertising and the rationalization of ruthless self-aggrandizement ("Sell the product!" "For the good of the corporation!" "Our stockholders deserve everything we can get for them!" "Our company— nation—parish—diocese—which stands for so much can do no less!"). Knowing my own propensities, and suspecting they are not peculiar to me, I fear these popular standards will soften or seduce the growing Underground Church even as they have long since corrupted the Establishment Churches.

More than anyplace else, I too now find the Church of the Christ I have long loved in the "small groups of intimate friends getting together. . . ." It is here I find not only expression of, but care for, the most powerful ideas and ideals that I have known. I still enjoy the ceremonies of the Churches, but I don't fancy the meanness, the politics, the lies (to themselves as well as to me and others), and the moral cowardice cloaked in the ceremonies.

A glance, a touch, a word, a meal shared, holding your wife's hand through the midnight phone calls promising the rape and death of "that little girl of yours"; walking together through the curses screamed by White housewives and through the spittle of filth-mouthing fuzz; surviving the cocktail-party contempt of suburbia; shared anguish with others and newfound strength to protest this grotesque war in which our President keeps us involved; bearing the humiliation with the few as the majority rationalizes its way toward more inaction: these are the truths of real life in Christ today, and the Underground Church has helped us confront and bear them when the Establishment has been silent or chiding.

So much hope and dedication is here, outside the formalized religious community. These clergy and laity have faced the prostitution of their simplistic, childhood faith and have accepted the fact that it all really did happen a long time ago. It's too late, now, to weep over what might have been; and these folk are far too given to making a positive difference in what God has given them to work with—the world as it is—to waste time enshrining and idolizing the nearly-successful failures of the past.

This isn't to say that it's easy. For one, I have imaged myself with a collar around my neck since the eleventh grade. And I have learned so much that is good from the Church, for which I shall always be grateful. But I am convinced that its present way is the way of death. I know of no other alternative than to look outside what has been for the meanings and means of expression that have been denied me (and so many others) within the seeming charity of popular religion.

People are shocked. Some with whom I have been privileged to share the moments of stress in past battles are quite fervent in their reactions to the decisions of a growing number of us to leave the usual work of the Establishment Church. They empathize with but deplore our callings into practical tasks in the real world.

I don't know! Even as I write these words, my supervisors in the ecclesiastical past are still justifying themselves with explanations that my attitudes and those of others recorded here are the inevitable result of personal instabilities and vocational failure. Certainly, they may be right; and I know this well. But some of us are willing to stake our futures, our families, and our own shattered dreams on a search for some-

thing else, for something more, believing that there is still reason and ability as well as hope left in us and that our calling *is*
of God as we go out into unknown newness.

My friend and longtime mentor, Joseph Fletcher (*Morals
and Medicine, Situation Ethics*[1]), recently said to me,

Zim, you've got to be free to do what you know you must do. God
never calls a man to do that which is totally unacceptable to him.
Decide what is right for you and your family and for your given
talents. What makes you happy will help you serve others . . . so,
do it! After all these years you're finding out that Christ's ministry
can take a man a long way away from the official Church.

And he's right. The Underground Church is made up of men
and women aware of a greater calling than their old denominational structures can seem to grasp.

For me, the call has led into the Peace Corps. Idealism,
practical effectiveness, honesty, imagination, responsible non-
conformity . . . these are the characteristics of our new life
that impress all of us who have just become members of the
staff. Of the thirteen of us now being trained, four are clergy,
three from the same Episcopal seminary. Literally, dozens of
clergy of all faiths have come this way; more are applying
right now. Roman Catholics, Protestants, Jews, and agnostics
equally seem to find encouragement, incentive, and opportunity here. I am not implying that the Peace Corps *is* the
Underground Church any more than such could be said about
the other government agencies to which the clergy and the
searching laity are now turning in pursuit of their vision of
themselves and their meaning in the world. Community Rela-

[1] Joseph Fletcher, *Morals and Medicine* (Beacon, Boston, 1960, paper);
Fletcher, *Situation Ethics: The New Morality* (Westminster, Philadelphia,
1966).

tions Service, Job Corps and affiliated agencies, VISTA, and others like these are the ones most sought out by Underground churchmen whom I know.

You see, in my experience, the strength to make the break —to ascertain the truth behind the pathetic charade of the Churches and to make the decision to go beyond it in my own life—that strength was born and nourished in the Underground Church. Obviously, the same thing is happening to others.

A friend in the ecclesiastical hierarchy bade me farewell with these words: "You have failed your job here, and you will fail again. You won't find the Peace Corps any more to your liking than you have found the Church. You will keep trying new jobs until there is no place left for you to go; nothing that you'll want, nothing that will want you."

He may be right. I am pretty well aware of my overidentification with the Black poor and of my increasingly forceful abhorrence of war, police brutality, corrupt politics, systemic racism, and money-grubbing religious structures. I know that I am disillusioned, pretty bitter, and perhaps paranoid. But I am also aware that my friend and others like him in the hierarchy *must* condemn the critics of the business that supports them. You know, it's like General Motors *had* to try to destroy Ralph Nader.

But if my friend (and I really do love this man) and his fellow institutionalists are wrong, his life and their lives are mocked. Therefore, they have to play it this way. Their rightness cannot bear questions or criticism. And being right, it is clean and economical to let me, and others like me, go, and go quickly.

So, I go! We go! They go . . . more and more.

There's a prayer I prayed once, and still do a lot, that I'd like to commend to my fellow churchmen underground:

I think
I'd rather be a fool for your sake
in the eyes of the world, Lord Christ,
than just a success . . .
I think.
Amen.

3/ Toward a United Peace and Freedom Church

by JOHN PAIRMAN BROWN

Today's novelty will of course turn out in the end to have been either temporary or permanent; either a frivolous variation on existing themes or an authentic phase of historical evolution; either a fad or a revolution. We have always got to reckon with the possibility that the most eccentric faddist has somehow latched onto what is in the wind and that the most serious ideologist or revolutionary or organizer is only shuffling the well-worn deck. It's a matter of discerning the spirits.

I guess two things distinguish the revolution from the fad. (1) The authentic revolution continues the arrow of previous development; it has a fulcrum in the past in order to exercise leverage on the future. And however violent the Damascus conversion of the revolutionary, the images of his childhood and the style of his former operation are continued in his new work. (2) The revolution is called into existence by the cry of radically new needs, or needs which have assumed a radically new urgency; the disparate human and organizational materials which make it up must be fused together in heat and implosion by the pressure of the future—the place where what we call God is. But there is no obvious formula by which to apply these standards. For the whole point of the revolution is that the new growth of the tree takes its set before it is obvious what is happening. The revolution or the revolutionary is only born in the first place by withdrawal or penetration into the secret place where our psyche vibrates in resonance with the world's new frequency.

Also the electric cable of history has two cords in it, one positive and one negative. Even when we have correctly judged that a revolution is in progress, or have allied ourselves with it, we still have to determine which side of the circuit it is on, whether it is basically fruitful or basically destructive or intrinsically ambivalent. To judge or operate on this level is the work of the saint.

But (we are told) we are entitled to wish that all the Lord's people were saints.

By "the Church" I mean the phase of Western society—really now of world society—which takes with radical seriousness the fact that we are children of Israel and brothers of Jesus. But I suggest also that we have not read the bible right if we fail to see that Achilles is a cousin of David, that Prometheus springs from the same spiritual impulse as Job, that Paul is an heir of Thucydides, that the Buddha is a mask of the Christ. It's not all that easy to cut ourselves off from the Church—not enough (for example) to secularize apocalypse with Marx or to announce the death of God. This is not just a definition I arbitrarily make; it is a claim for the radical unity of planetary culture—since at our best we are men of goodwill, trying in our action and symbolic forms to make sense of the one cosmos—and in particular a claim that Jesus is toward the center of that unity.

More precisely, that he *is* that unity.

As we all know, the Church which the sociologist sees in America is on the whole an amenity of suburbia. Of course, the power represented by suburbia makes it possible for us to vacation in Lake Tahoe or the Greek islands or Tahiti, commute to Washington, and go to world conferences in Khartoum. But suburbia is the place out of which we do those things and back to which we go. We all also know what sort of job or inheritance we have to hold to stay in suburbia.

Suburbia understandeth all things and pardoneth all things. If the penitent revolutionary shows up with the right inheritance or the right job, suburbia—the inner suburbia of the soul—is always glad to let bygones be bygones and kill the fatted calf. Not because it is threatened, but because it is realistic. It understands very clearly the sacrament of affluence. Our willingness to go back to Spruce Terrace with no questions asked is by itself the outward and visible sign of the inward and spiritual grace which I can only define in Movement language: finking out.

I write here under the proviso that the meaning of Jesus is active reconciling nonviolence. The world is in no doubt on this point, which would seem to come through pretty transparently from the Gospels; only the Church has from time to time raised doubts. The sanction which the New Testament puts behind nonviolence is the imminent end of the world; not merely our death, or the death of this or that society, but the death of human society and its environment together. Until recently this was interpreted as at worst error, as at best symbolism. We are now aware that it may be simply prophecy: the prophets took sin so seriously that they believed it would have to involve the possibility of pulling down the roof over our heads. Now that we know there is in fact a mechanism by which this may happen, it would seem as if the new age which has begun in our lifetime and will persist for the foreseeable future is one that the gospel applies to more directly than we had thought likely. The last days are upon us—in the sense that violence has priced itself out of the market, it has gotten too big for this planet, and the beatitudes appear not so much as idealism, but rather as simple good sense.

We do not simply live in a time of novelties; we surmise that a principle of novelty has been built into history for a long time coming up. I have taken it for granted that our life in the Church—which means our life at its center, since we cannot alter the fact of our history—will also have to enter a new phase. If we choose to try and avoid copping out, we can't avoid the burden of judging whether this or that current novelty is destined for obsolescence or permanence: whether it is fad or revolution. I said that the novelty must have a staging area in the past from which to march into the future. I suggest that this firm base is provided by return to the example and spirit of the authentic Jesus: a more-than-Reformation which can liberate us into the glorious freedom of the children of God.

I said that the bona fide revolution must also come from a radical urgency in the present. I guess we all know where it's really *at* today: that the oppressed of four continents have decided not to be kicked around any longer. (For charity's sake I leave Europe out of account, although we would also have to ask what is going on in Portugal or Rumania.) Many of us can personally testify that in various parts the United States has gotten a reputation, apparently well-deserved, for suppressing that cry against injustice. So I take it that the single question which is set in all our examination booklets is this: How can we as the Church (that is, as persons in community radically conscious of our history), in the spirit of Jesus' loving nonviolence, come to terms with the worldwide revolution against injustice?

As soon as we look at the hopeless magnitude of the job through the eyes of the black militant in the American urban

ghetto or the guerrilla fighter in Vietnam; as soon as we think
of the actual conditions of conflict in which the rebellion must
maintain itself—and we must think of those things—the idea
of nonviolence acquires a sheen of tinsel irrelevance. The one
platform which unites H. Rapp Brown and Lyndon Johnson,
General Westmoreland and Ho Chi Minh is that guns are
necessary. "Violence is as American as blueberry pie." We
have heard at least enough of each party denouncing the violence of his opposite number. It takes one to tell one. The
pacifist is criticized for not criticizing the violence of groups
with which he may find himself in uneasy coalition, for sully-
ing the purity of his witness. His answer to *this* question is
simple. The criticism of violence is in competent hands; all the
others are tumbling over each other in eagerness to make it
their vocation; he is thereby liberated to make something else
his *thing*. But he still has to demonstrate how constructive
nonviolence is *necessary* and *possible* in a world of armed
revolution and counterrevolution.

Necessary. As we try to make the scene where the future
already exists in the present determinations of men's hearts,
we see immediately that this landscape of the imagination is
dominated by the possibility of the nuclear cloud, the deadly
toadstool, growing out of the corruption of living impulses,
which bids fair to poison the picnic party in the forest of this
planet. And we know that we do not know which aggression
of ours or our enemy will make it sprout and which will not.
We see once more that as we were told long ago, the only way
to begin the new way is to begin it; it can only grow from a
seed like itself. Reading history, we see suddenly that some of
the revolutions of our time will succeed, and someday the
affairs of men will be ruled from Harlem or Havana or Hanoi.
We are tempted to make excuses for the revolutionaries, to
make allowances for those who are ungentle today so that

gentleness may be possible tomorrow. But we really know that the child is father to the man. We can trace the global damage Americans are doing to the insistence of our fathers on clearing out a few aborigines so that the great theocratic experiment could take place under perfect conditions, with a clean slate. The Negro or the Latin American or the Vietnamese is not a different breed from us—he was programmed from the same tape. We have no reason to doubt that his victory, on present principles, will presumably generate new oppressed peoples, lying under the same threat of ecological destruction. Nothing but the best will do.

Possible. I say then that nonviolence is necessary. How is it possible? In the first place, it is not something which we can advocate vicariously for somebody else. Perhaps we can let our suffering stand for him; but by the same token only he, never we, can let his suffering stand for us. Here is the point where the ease of finking out that I have spoken of is so critical. For *a bourgeois pacifist is a phony.* I say this in full awareness that most pacifists are bourgeois like myself. Phoniness (as St. Paul pointed out long ago) is endemic in the human situation. I write this uncomfortable stuff once again to give myself reason for continuing (or better, for beginning) to lay myself on the line. So far as we acquiesce to our membership in the bourgeoisie, we have tacitly connived at the fruits of violence—stock-dividends, social status. Only so far as we have succeeded in making contact somewhere with the oppressed, tying our lot to theirs so that in some real way we rise and fall with them, have we any right to investigate the creative possibilities of love in their situation. The theist affirms that there are no moral boxes in the universe, and with fear and trembling we assent. We will affirm that we will never come into a cul-de-sac, that with imaginative sympathy we can always find a line which is at once ethical and fruitful. But we will also affirm that the very first act of imaginative sympathy must be bona fide dialog with the oppressed, a dialog which is an actual living with him. Our circle of sympathy will never swell to embrace more than a tiny part of those who deserve it. The only possibility of our justification is the constancy of our effort to enlarge that sympathy. The definition of finking out is "to rest on our oars." "Call no man blessed until he is dead."

We have all read about the Civil Rights movement and the Peace movement. If two years ago we were persuaded that nonviolence was necessary and possible in them, that somewhere in this area lay the central moral act of our time, by now we should have made actual contact with those movements. If we have not, probably now would be a good time to stop reading this piece and do so.

Let me transcribe a current injustice so far unspoken for, in hopes that somebody will want to make it his thing. On August 18, 1967, a Shoshone Indian, Rich Williams, who refused to "fight the white man's war in Vietnam," was sentenced to five years' hard labor by a general court-martial in the Presidio of San Francisco. He claimed that by the treaty of Ruby Valley, October 1, 1863, the Shoshone nation was recognized by the Army in terms of peace and friendship, and that no true Shoshone voted in the white man's election. Chief Rolling Thunder of the Shoshone, having taken his oath by holding a white eagle feather in his hand, testified on Williams' behalf.

We Indians are the keepers of this land. You notice we don't say owners—we say keepers. The Great Spirit owns this land. If the white man wishes to live in peace and plenty on this continent, he must not upset the forces of nature. We Indians live in accordance with these forces of nature and understand them. There may be earthquakes, there may be floods. . . . The writings say that if the white man does not correct himself, a gourd of ashes will be dropped on this land and all of us will suffer. The Shoshone are peaceful. When will the white man learn his ways?

The red man has not even got going for him what the black man has: no militants, no violence, only Buffie Sainte-Marie, the sweet singer of Canaan—"My country 'tis of thy people I'm dying." Thomas Merton and others have written perceptively of the Shoshone recently, and I hope somebody will take over where my habitual rhetoric fails me, and I find my mouth opening and shutting like a fish. The Church's habitual rhetoric failed it long ago. And this is why the bulk of the Peace and Civil Rights movements dropped the Church like a hot potato long ago: not being historians and yet judging the Church by what they actually saw, they took Jesus too seriously to be able to call themselves Christians. But the existence of the movements has conversely preached the gospel to the Church.

We may think of what are called the Churches—better "denominations"—as spread out, sitting in a spectrum before us like parties in the French Parliament from left to right, with the understanding that the ostensible ideological differences are things which the better thinkers in all the denominations do not take with full seriousness. (Class and national differences are now—in many cases always have been—a deeper line of fracture.) But in view of the claim of the Peace and Freedom movements to authentic moral reality—*the* moral reality of our time—a radical regrouping of the ecclesiastical parliament has taken place. The front rows have been gotten off their duffs and have started to walk forward. They are now facing an actual job to be done, and as they march into the apex of the pie-slice, the front-to-back divisions between them are wiped out. But if they look back, they can see a widening gap between their united front and the sulky isolation of the

denominational bodies stranded from the new thing and from
each other.

At this point I make contact with the theme of our book;
and I claim that the operative growing edge of the Underground Church is that regrouping of lines which the Peace and
Freedom movements have brought about in the denominational spectrum.

If, as we are told, God cares for justice—a better way to say
this would be that concern for justice is the definition of service of God—it becomes plain that the Peace and Freedom
movements, certainly at least insofar as they are nonviolent,
are an incognito part of the Church. But the very essence of
the Christ is his incognito; Messiahship consists in refusing to
be Messiah: "When saw we thee hungered and fed thee?" And
it is enough for the servant to be as his master. If the definition
of the Christ is his incognito, his Body can happily accept the
same status. That does not mean the theologian is out of a
job—he is the instructed scribe who brings out of his treasure
things old and new. Rather *the function of the Underground
Church is to define the Peace and Freedom movements as
the true Church*—to give them explicitly the ideology on
which they had implicitly been working all along. This function, like other functions, is not the whole show, but it's not
contemptible either.

There must be a convergence among the denominations in
the permanent unchanging concerns of the Church—of humanity: family life, the preservation of the natural environment, the truth about the cosmos, art and music, the conduct
of the common meal, the search of every individual for himself. And, of course, each of those permanent concerns has a
new-color light thrown on it by the radical changes of our age.
I am confining myself to the regrouping produced directly by
those radical changes themselves.

Church unity has been the concern of Christians for most of this century. The closest thing we have seen to the right thing has been the formation of the united Church of South India in response to the scandal presented to Hinduism by Christian disunity. Here, as in other aspects of social renewal, the rest of the world has been ahead of the West. We are after all committed to the belief that Church renewal is the heart of social renewal. Among us Church reunion has been something discussed up in the stratosphere—or let us say up there in the back benches of our ecclesiastical parliament where the bureaucrats sit. Characteristic is the Consultation on Church Union now going on between the hierarchies of the American denominations of the center. They are still patching over the differences created by the Reformation, differences which nobody takes with full seriousness except as obstacles to reunion. But the real obstacles to reunion are the things which the COCU does not discuss because it takes them for granted: that the proposed united Church will be American and middle-class, a coalition of white moderates and Uncle Toms.

But incautiously the ecumenists have also asked for grass-roots concern, grass-roots action, grass-roots mission. And I say, "While you slept, the thing you were talking about has already come into being among people who were fixing their attention on something else, *because* they were fixing their attention on something else." Unity is the product of concern for justice and truth, it is not the product of concern for unity. It is the Underground Peace and Freedom Church which is carrying out the characteristic necessary moral act of our times, which is speaking the name of Jesus to those who have been touched by the spirit of Jesus. Now we present the ecclesiastical Establishment with a *fait accompli;* the thing which they are planning to do has come into existence under their eyes. We are happy to give them any credit for it they care to take. If they do not like the form it has assumed, let them at least not reproach us for failing to take them with sufficient seriousness.

I was in Beirut at the time of Selma, and when I came back to the States, I asked one of my students who had been in Selma what he had found there. "The primitive Church." I think of Father Daniel Berrigan—at Selma, making contact (while under discipline) with the revolutionaries and renewal of Latin America, joining the black Catholics of South Africa on Good Friday in mourning the death of our tribal chief. I think of the Free Church on Telegraph Avenue in Berkeley, founded by my former student Dick York, bringing hippies and the Peace movement together in a common format, giving radical Pentecostals and radical Catholics the common liturgy of finding housing, finding food, finding people. In the Depression the ancestor of many of these movements was the Catholic Worker group with its houses of hospitality across the country, giving a practical witness to poverty and peace. The Civil Rights movement was most itself—or so it seems—in temporary groupings. Currently—at least for the time being—it has been taken over by black militants who are unwilling to renounce violence. Many of us do not consider ourselves in a position to denounce them; but we can imagine situations where we could no longer walk beside them. Thus, after this long hot summer of '67—which bids fair to engross every season of the year—even though at bottom we know that *nigger* and *napalm* define phases of a single historical event, it is the urgency of Vietnam which most radically is pushing men of goodwill into a single camp.

What I have seen as the characteristic form of the Underground Church is the gathering together of Catholics, Anglicans, Protestants, and followers of Jesus (baptized or unbaptized) in a common meal—because it is the only way they

have been able to find the strength of community for the job
that faced them tomorrow. Sometimes that common meal has
taken the form of a traditional liturgy, or an experimental
liturgy, or a completely free liturgy, or a sharing of bread and
wine, or of coffee and doughnuts; I am not able to make any
sharp distinctions among these even if I wished to. When it has
been a liturgy, more or less, there has never been any question
about the validity of any minister present; it is taken for
granted that if he is authorized in his own denomination and
chooses to be present, he is the representative of Christ. As a
matter of course, all the ministers present concelebrate, although this is irregular for the Anglicans and illegal in Canon
Law for the Romans.

We have had these common meals in parish houses, in private homes in the suburbs, in the ghetto, in houses of hospitality, in jail, outside San Quentin during an execution, on the
Capital steps at Sacramento while capital punishment was
being debated, on the vigil line at Port Chicago while the
napalm trucks rolled by. Others can tell where they have gathered together. Above all, there has been no question of the
meaning of what was done—the argument over which so
many barrels of ink have been spilled during the Reformation,
the Counterreformation, the Ecumenical movement, the
Councils. Because the meaning was defined in every man's
heart to his own satisfaction by the common purpose, the job
in hand.

The whole Underground Church bag is different from the
sectarianism of the radical Reformation and the American
frontier in one critical respect: there is no intention whatever
of forming a new Church. The token of this is that there is
never any question of informal ordination of ministers. The
clergy in the movement are children each of their own
Churches; it is through those Churches that we first learned

Christ. There is an exact parallel here to the Peace movement generally, which operates by coalition among representatives of various groups, with the universal presumption that proselytism is ruled out of the question. In fact, as I say, there is a sense in which the renewed Church and the Peace movement are the same thing. To the extent that we have formulated our aim, we intend to surface as a nucleus of Church union and renewal, in the hope that what we represent will melt the denominations from the bottom up. If we meet an Establishment ecumenism painfully trying to push its way down, so much the better; but if we want something to boil, it's always the bottom of the kettle to which we apply heat. If we like, we could say that for its ministry the Underground Church exists parasitically on the Establishment. But I can point out that theological seminaries overseas rely parasitically for their faculties on Western graduate seminaries—and that still the overseas Churches have moved ahead of us.

What of a true Church is lacking in the nascent groupings which I have described? Of course, it doesn't have church architecture; but then neither does America have a church architecture, apart from the white steeples of New England. It doesn't have a national hierarchy or a budget; indeed, it has come into being in despair at the unresponsiveness of hierarchies and budgets. But it does not allow women and children to go hungry, and it can raise thousands for bail when it is needed. It has a theology, of which the kind reader has a sampling in his hands, and which can make some claim to have rescued forgotten truths. It has the only indigenous music American Christianity ever had, the music of the Negro and the frontiersman, and it has made its own additions. Unlike American Christianity, it has had its martyrs and saints.

The one thing which is lacking so far is a definition of family life as Christian. To a large extent this is a reflection of the stresses of the Peace movement, which favor the unmarried, those with casual liaisons, Catholic celibates, the divorced, little old ladies in tennis shoes. Lest this be thought a criticism, it is simply intended as a translation of St. Paul's recommendations to the Church at Corinth.

But in turn, all this is due to the difficulty of family life in America generally: the grandmother-centered family of the ghetto; the Plexiglass bubble over the suburban home; with the reverse of the coin, the loving squalor of Haight-Ashbury or Greenwich Village. And this in turn is associated with our failure of attitude toward the land: the cancer of urban agglomerations and freeways, the destruction of the natural balance, the impossibility of humane farming. We have treated nature with the same callousness as we have treated the nature-peoples—the red man, the black man, the yellow man —and should not be surprised when breakdown there is reflected in breakdown where we cannot get away from biology: in our families. Family renewal would be the beginning of planetary renewal.

When I came into the Church as a kind of adult, it was mysteriously clear to me that the Episcopal Church in these United States was where I belonged. It is still clear to me that when I or mine get married and buried, I want it done in my Church's way and not some other way. In Beirut I couldn't find the Church I knew in the available British military chapel (or elsewhere). Wherever I have been in the United States, there has always been an Episcopal parish available where there was an actual beginning of different kinds of people getting together—either because it was the only parish in town or because it was on the wrong side of the tracks. I suppose others more or less, each in his own way, can make some such confession for their own denominations.

But (apart from being married and buried as Thomas

Cranmer willed it) so far as I personally and, I guess, my wife are concerned, we would be willing to turn from the Sunday-morning formalism to the Saturday-night informalism, not without a real sense of loss, of breaking old ties, but also with a positive sense of conviction. But the Saturday-night informalism still isn't a suitable format for the kids. It seems as if they have to go through the same evolution we did. This is what holds us attached to both the old and the new—at least until the new way is willing to develop in ways which so far it has not done.

When we came back to the United States in '65, the kids as a solid block of four musketeers from nine to four years old took on *Church* as a project. One pretended he wasn't part of the family until he had a chance to appear in a little alb. One was willing to go if we could promise that the *Benedictus* in which his name appeared would be used. One looks forward to another Sunday in which her name will again appear in the Psalm, "everlasting Joy and Felicity." One practices reading, following the Propers with a grubby thumb (unless the Revised Standard Version is substituted). The evenings when mummy's and daddy's friends come in have their own attractions, like dusting off the big coffee-urn, but they are not Church in quite the same way. What would have to happen for family people to be able to go over entirely to the Underground Church, for it to become fully what it is now potentially at best, that is, an actual family of the faithful? I think I can suggest an answer in two equivalent forms, a sacramental form and a psychological form.

(1) Even though the Underground Church is "parasitic" on the established Church for its ministry, it would have to become autonomous in the matter of baptism. (Perhaps marriage also, but this raises legal questions, and the essential points are covered by considering baptism.) Here and there

we have seen or heard of movement people having their kids
baptized ecumenically—which is irregular or illegal, at
least if Catholics and Protestants take part. What I have not
seen is the baptism of adults taking place in the same kind of
context. In part this is because of the nonproselytism of the
movement; in part it is because the new groupings of Christians have not realized that they are becoming the Church,
have not thought to make available to their new associates the
good thing they themselves have received—the possibility of a
fresh start.

(2) On the fringes of society what we are accustomed to
see is people treating fads as if they were revolutions—in art,
music, drug-taking, fashion, etc. I suggest that the nascent
reunited Church within the movement has made the opposite
mistake: it has not yet fully waked up, opened its eyes to the
new world into which it is being born, and so treats in the
aspect of a fad what is really a revolution. Everywhere else the
vain winds of false doctrine or faddism are supreme, and secretly everybody knows that today's revelation is tomorrow's
drag and day-after-tomorrow's camp. Out of force of habit we
treat the cooperation of Christians in the movement with the
same frivolousness. But if we try and enter down into the
secret places of our psychology or think about our knowledge
of history, we truly know that the pressures which have
brought us together are permanent ones. If the Vietnam horror is patched up five or ten or fifteen years from now—if
things go on that long—we will get into the same bag somewhere else, unless the Johnsons and McNamaras and Rusks
undergo a change of heart, which we must presume would be
a long-term business. If the rebellions of '67 can be swept
under the rug by suitably calculated concessions, the massive
apathy and injustice of America will remain. We ought to

decide that the new groupings which have been forced on us by the power of history or the Spirit are a lifetime affair—an affair of generations or centuries—and rearrange our lives accordingly.

I do not know what would be a sufficient impulse to push us over the threshhold of baptism into a renovated Community. It might seem most plausible that a single prophetic voice is required, another Luther. Each man involved in the Underground Church, if he is honest with himself in his heart, apparently at the moment is deciding that the job is not for *him*—whether out of fear or self-knowledge. Barriers are being broken through most evidently in tongue-speaking or the hippie Free Church; but each of these seems ever so slightly too sectarian to give the cue to the whole Church. A friend of mine is contemplating a new ecumenical mendicant order. Perhaps it is possible that the new thing will spring up spontaneously in different places at once, a polygenesis; but evolution and history indicate alike that a new birth has a single father.

This inconclusive discussion suggests that the new thing will happen when it will happen, by people who (perhaps) had their eye on something else, and that our job is to work toward the right thing in what seems at the moment the best way, while at the same time keeping our eyes open for the likelihood of its happening somewhere else in another way. Perhaps organizationally one preliminary task still remains to be done.

Unsystematically inside the denominations and within various umbrellas over the denominations, fellowships dedicated to peace or social justice have come into being. Quite properly each of them has entered into coalition to some degree with the larger secular groups devoted to the same thing. But the Christian fellowships have been too presumptuous and too timid, have missed their true function by overshooting and undershooting. They have been presumptuous in talking as if they were the Church, by entering into coalition only with vaguely religious or politically moderate groups, and by not seeing that God (who acts where he decides to act) has called the movement as a whole, and in particular its radically non-violent and radically committed phase, precisely to *be* his Church, to do the thing that the Churches as such have failed to do. But at the same time the Christian fellowships have been too timid. Out of personal uncertainty and false humility they have ceased to believe that through no merit of their own they hold in their hands a treasure which no man should willingly forgo. They should see their task to be baptizing the movement into unity, giving it the joy and long-range certainty which it doesn't have now: bringing the explicit name of Christ to what is already implicitly his Body.

To this end we perhaps need a *Christian Peace and Freedom Congress*. Any person or group that accepted the formula of the Call would be welcome to come. The agenda of the Congress would simply be to state that the reunion of the Church had already taken place, and, therefore, that it was not proclaiming the formation of a new sect but the actual unity of the existing denominations; further, it would invite persons and groups inside or outside the existing Churches who agreed with it in its estimate of the situation to join it. America is unique enough in its apostasy so that when we have begun settling things at home, there will be time enough to approach the Churches overseas in penitence and reparation. It is true that an Underground Church so formed would have within it the seeds of becoming a new Establishment. So did the twelve apostles.

One mark of the true Church at all times and places is the

forked road before it, leading to a right way and a wrong way. This is just the human situation as Robert Frost saw it: "Two roads lay in a wood"; better that than the full-blown irreparable corruption or petrifaction which seems to be the single current alternative—and a real and plausible one.

4/ Diary
from the Underground

by *DANIEL BERRIGAN, S.J.*

October 29th. Suppose after all, that *were* the way to win? I think of M., younger than myself, a grandee graced with assurance, color, energy. His life level as a plumb line. He has a future in the Church.

Is that the way to win? The question goes out like the hand of an infant, blind, instinctual, as though the shape of life were the shape of a full breast. Or as though a man's arm were to terminate in an infant's hand.

October 30th. To deny that life's juices are milk is not to assert that they are gall. Quite the contrary.

Sixty percent of one's life these days passes for living. Which is to say, it is not capable of passion or compassion. We are sick at heart at the reverberation of bombs on distant villages. We are hiding out; our world is in flames.

What is my life capable of? Tell me, my brother! The heart's unkillable outcry. The clamor it raises, more terrible than the cry of "fire!" raised at midnight in a house of sleeping children.

A man thought he was in hell. But his neighbor, looking out from his own suffering, saw this other infirmary. *O beatitudo!* At least he has made it!

Signs observed along the roads of hell; try our retirement plan, try our beer, try our—. A definition of heaven: a place free of big claims.

November 1st. "Where there is enough faith, there will be enough doubt" (Zen).

We need our doubts as we need our faith, so that faith may be, not a dead center, but a point of departure, like Abraham's. So that it may have both center and circumference, like the faith of Paul. So that we may live at the edge, and dislocate our selfishness and idolatry, and may at length even include man in God, where life is.

Enough doubt to keep faith on the move.

Enough faith so that doubt may have a direction.

Enough doubt so that faith may be marked by intellectual passion.

Enough faith so that doubt may be contained.

Enough doubt so that faith may not be housebroken or castrated or forbidden the real world.

November 2nd. Not to turn from suffering, but to "turn" suffering in a new direction. This is to personalize it by giving it over, and by receiving light which the person alone can shed on it. In such a way, one liberates its mystery and renders modest its problematic. Mystery: the crisis of broken or renewed relationships. Problematic: a question of quanta (how much, how long?) or of psychology (will this destroy or restore me, how best to deal with it?).

The absurdity of an "explanation" of suffering to which the mystery of the cross is sometimes reduced. "Presto," the cross explains. Which, of course, is just what the cross forever refuses to do: to be a stage construct, an excuse for a drama of defeat.

Lord, with regard to my brother,
          Let me
          down
          not
          lightly.

November 4th. An act of faith: not to be able to measure the good that we do. An equal act of faith: to be able to measure so bitterly the evil that we do.

During the war, we could not win games or create art or go on vacation without a tic of bad conscience. And yet, for all the closure of human possibility, we knew ourselves as never before.

November 7th. For some of us, peace became the integrating task of existence. We did not choose the task; the task enlisted us. And it was to our shame that as the years mounted and the fury grew, we were not waging peace with the same ingenuity and persistence and skill with which some were waging war.

At the same time, we found it almost impossible to live "normally," to conceive what liturgy might be, or authority, or community, as long as the innocent were being destroyed. We did not know what these things could mean, when these things were silent about the life around us. And as far as ourselves were concerned, we could not undertake good housekeeping in the Church, while murder was occurring down the street.

And even in our blindness and perplexity we were working, so we thought, for the good name and honor of the Church.

November 10th. It occurred to me once, that the opposite of poetry was prose. The two shared honors as ways or forms apt to convey certain aspects of the truth. Both were useful, both had a long history in every culture.

God had used both to convey his love, his beauty, and his truth.

Now we must, however, speak otherwise. The opposite of poetry is no longer prose. It is the sound of the gears of Juggernaut. Or it is the rhetoric of executioners. Or it is silence; the silence of emptiness and panic, the silence of the death of God, which sucks into its void all the foul proliferation of power, politics and murder and lies and justified violence and neglect of the innocent.

In such an age, poetry will still exist. But it will go underground.

Prose also must be content with a minority status, where it is to exist at all. For who really is capable of conveying the prosaic truth about man and his world today? And is it possible for this skill to be aligned with power, money, rhetoric, security? When and how did we last hear the truth, and from whom? The question is not a form of cynicism or despair.

"The great task of man is not to serve the lie" (Parin).

November 13th. The feeling of being under sentence probably has something to do with the uncertainties of war. Much more, with solidarity toward all those under the bombs, and toward those whose lives have become a great NO to social contracts which make the bombs inevitable.

And I wonder, (1) How men can be unconscious when consciousness is a synonym for human survival? (2) How men who are so cut off from reality can so quickly mobilize to destroy me? The "good man" becomes murderous in his sleep.

Old barriers and norms are down. The ex-nun marries a priest. And the community celebrates at a Eucharist. No one knows if the new thing will work; the evidence is not in yet. What we know very well is that there is little of the old forms that works at all for anyone but the lawyers and the taxider-mists.

April 15th. Not much to be said about oneself, as one stands under judgment. Waiting to be dealt with, for one's case to be called. Or more, like an animal in a pound. Not much is going for me; except maybe the truth, the truth of the damned, the truth of the innocent, the truth of a wave that is gathering strength, steeling itself. The times alone can tell. A man is required to be ready, and to know that he can never be ready. He can only hope and work for the inner cleanliness that makes him less unready for "the hour" (St. John).

April 18th. A Poetry Reading tonight. As one grows older and skinnier, the young seem to be more carnivorous. At least one hopes to have some meat to offer them! The sight of such innocence, and one's own helplessness to offer anything except the frailest of bulwarks against a vicious future. What is left? The possibility of love and communion. These students will have so little else; but what else is there after all?

November 21st. A long session with B. D. He has left the priesthood to marry, and has heard no single word from his superiors, either of blessing or of condemnation. They evidently intend this silence as an act of official protest against his "sin." They take no account, of course, of the angry scandal awakened in young people in crisis, when the Church offers no inkling of the compassion of Christ.

November 25th. It struck me that the saying of Gandhi, "purify the means," applies rigorously to my situation. In order to be present and available as a man of change, I must have mastered the ordinarily crippling personal needs of man. However genuine and legitimate in fact, these needs would impede me in what I have proposed to do with my life—a kind of public action (*Leiturgia*) for men. The purpose may indeed be so pure that the Church can as yet only turn away from it with a howl of recognition. But the means must be pure. Otherwise the source of action and passion is polluted.

I want to present myself for crisis, as one presents himself for his wedding day—in joy, in fearful joy, in joy which casts out fear. Is this possible? I only know that the longing arises in me.

December 1st. It is entirely possible that I will not survive this war as a Jesuit, as events make clear. But this is the best equivalent, I think, to what a soldier must prepare himself for, as he is ordered to the front. I too have been ordered to a front—and I know cold sweat and fear and sleepless nights. I must trust, as any green draftee, that I am going in a good cause. But I cannot be certain. And no one can go in my place. My contract, my life itself, is being annulled by the times. New vows are being written in the blood of my brothers, even though the Church refuses to accept these commitments. But infinitely more of my life goes into these vows than I could have summoned when I first pronounced vows as a Jesuit, at 20. Perhaps it is all one and the same process. And perhaps what I said then led like a shot arrow to this. I vowed to stand for life, to resist death, to shield the innocent and house the poor and confront the powers hostile to Christ. And now mankind itself is arising to conduct me into "more stately mansions, O my soul."

December 3rd. "That which is possible is inevitable." I think so too. The worst, the outer edge of life has to be traversed, paced off, known as carefully as one's own living room, its unfamiliarity and terror subdued. The worst, in the sense that life awaits one as the unknown, is inevitable. It is a fertile field that demands a harvest. But the worst is also the best. Call it providence.

December 4th. For me, the question "How real is Christ?" has melded with the question "How real is your brother?" While the weirdest rumors circulate about me, I have the option now of remaining at peace. I sense that my battle is as solitary as David Miller's, and may well end as his has up to now: judged by bankrupt Catholic liberals as being "useless," "noxious," "making claims on the law which are impossible to the law." The point being that Jesus himself *was* guilty according to law. The law here is embodiment of a climate of mind, which coalesces in certain murderous taboos. To pass beyond them *was* to court death; the law *was* violated. The sole justification is his appeal to life, to transcendence, to a remote ideal rendered less remote by the love that marked his life and death.

December 8th. When I faced the judge at the trial of David Miller and spoke, I felt a kind of tingling sense of recognition. I had heard and seen such a man before, had stood before him and pleaded my case—and had lost, inevitably. Sometime, the sacred claims a superior existence, appealing to a God who makes no severe demands on egoism. But the genuinely sacred begins humbly from the facts of sin, the omnipresence of death, and gently announces the rising of the waters, a heightened possibility, a love which is never quite defeated.

December 9th. The scandal I live with tonight—a Church wherein, in the space of a year since my exile, nothing has happened. Authorities still meet in secret, judge a man, condemn him with methods based on corrupt public relations. How does one live in a Church where claims to renewal are sedulously "updated," where progressivist language is a kind of new way of consuming the truth, where human rights are at a stalemate? Is the Church perpetually to be a non-happening? I can scarcely grow used to it. My own blood courses onward, my body builds on itself, newness breaks forth like a miracle, the imagination casts its nets and takes its soundings and draws in its rainbow fish.

I feel on the edge of one of those momentous crises which shatter the past like a pure note striking on crystal.

I am waiting, in a kind of calm of spirit, for "the Cossacks and the Holy Ghost" (Bloy).

The time is past when men can communicate with men by words alone. What is required of us is a covenant with death, which will be a great *yes* to life. A few men, who will "pass over," will stand up after death and speak to us from that favored geography of the other side.

December 12th. The anguish of Catholics who a few short years ago were secure and serene in their parishes, with their local interests and Catholic action. What a change! "What has happened? Do the bishops have the least inkling of our suffering? Do they know of our despair, of the faith and security that have vanished like a snow, of the enormous gap, widening each day, between expectation and fulfillment in the Church?"

December 13th. The gnawing temptation which seems to stalk my life, as a man-eater follows the spoor of a starving man. What if this great Claimant of history, so proudly attending man at every stage of his existence, as midwife, nurse, confidante, benefactor, lover, spouse, advocate—what if these proud names were but one side of a dark reality, an omnipresent evil, a shadowing and unshakable devil of dawn and noonday? The domination and power which claim man's conscience, energy, discipline, which awaken his fear, follow his footsteps with a trail of fire, refuse him all peace and spontaneity and natural integrity and sexual joy. Suppose this were the institutionalized seizure of man by his own fear, his immaturity, his psychic darkness, the perfect brush salesman, the iceman who cometh, the science fiction monster, the Freudian nightmare? Suppose that in order to be himself at least in some measure, some stature, man must strike beyond, and topple this one, the idol and ape of truth?

The past days are isolating the temptation as no other days have done. I will make my way through this nightmare only by a gift which I cannot even name as yet—a sixth sense that will help me to distinguish Hydra from reality. And so I pray.

If it is impossible, in a religious order, to do those things which mature men are doing on behalf of life, of the innocent, of decency and justice—one asks, is not such an order writing its own obituary?

December 14th. Visionaries who stay with men.

Men who stand by their vision.

"A modest Utopia" (Camus).

December 15th. The people who had been with Christ were continually talking about him. This accounts for the crowd who went out to him, for they had heard that he had given a sign. Seeing this, the Pharisees remarked to one another, "You see, there's nothing we can do. The whole world is running after him."

"Jesus told them, 'The time has come for the son of man to be glorified. I tell you unless a grain of wheat falls into the earth and dies, it remains a single grain. But if it dies, it brings a good harvest.' "

December 16th. Overheard somewhere: so I said to him, well if you really want to do something, you'd better go ahead and do it. I mean get married, or build a house, or start a child, or fly a kite. You'd better buy back or steal back that pound of flesh someone carved out of you and is keeping in escrow in deep freeze in a blood bank tabernacle somewhere as insurance against your running off with God's wife or the bank funds or the widow's glands. Or else it doesn't figure. You let the pound go, you'll never be whole again. Or the big butcher comes back for another steak and then another, because he hears you grow human meat. You're too damn healthy for his sick sacred peace of mind, he'd better plunge in and get a little reminder of whose kid you are. And before death you begin to look something like the turkey that the Happy American Family from Grandma Carnivore to Baby Eyetooth made sport of at our annual Thank-You-God. When the priests are going to head shrinkers to shed their bad-boy thoughts and the head shrinkers are going to the ostrich farms to take lessons in how to hide out, the rest of us are merely doing what Grandma told Mother good girls always do, which is to lie down and pay up. What a way to come—or go! I think Jesus puts a cattle prod to all the death-choosing victims huddled like castrated Brahmin bulls, their roar going up to high C before the facts of life. Which are: live it up, louse it up, jump once clicking heels three times, grasp the fakir's invisible rope and go straight off the pad, get lost, we need the graveyard space. . . .

December 18th. Is it possible that never having touched evil, I should never touch goodness?

History has a way of winnowing lives. The question now put to the German Church about her history in the thirties is not, "Why did a few men do maladroit or ill-timed things?" The real question is, "Why did the vast majority of men do nothing at all?" The absurd question put to me today reverses this order entirely.

I submit that it is almost impossible to administer the sacra-

ments according to the intention of Christ, without breaking
the law of the Church.

Sources of trouble: (1) trying to do thoughtfully all the
things one is supposed to do thoughtlessly; (2) playing a de-
lightful substitution game, strictly forbidden by the canons,
strictly recommended by the sources; that is to say, acts instead of words, faces instead of abstractions, flesh instead of
hideaway chastity.

December 19th. Let us pray. My Lord, may these weeks
ahead be steadfast in their dignity and courage. And may what
I am entering upon be a service to others, especially to the
victims of war, and to the victims of normalcy. Purify my
heart and my lips. Amen.

December 21st. Question: How long does it take a man to
come to a decision about his life?

Or to put the same thing in a different way, a student once
asked me, How long did it take to write this poem? Answer:
forty-five years. All my life and every plenary act. I cannot
ravel and unravel.

December 28th. The almost infinite capacity of some forms
of religion for alienation of conscience. I drove back from a
wedding with a young Catholic. He told me with obvious
relish that he had read, or supposed he had read, somewhere
that the Russians were prepared to lock up dope addicts who
violated "treatment." Finally, they were prepared to put to
death those who showed no capacity for "improvement."

This was recounted with a sanctimonious air of one who
could count on instant approval. Somewhat as though he had
been sharing a morsel of gossip about choir members in a
nineteenth-century rural parish.

It was galling to realize that he expected approval of me.

And that he looked for the approval of his Church toward the murderous methods of reducing humankind to onekind—his and my own.

December 29th. When I read of what has been done to the children in the Vietnam war, I am consumed with a bitter wonder at the "normal" life I have been leading for so long. And along with others. One religious leader, a respected liberal theologian, insists that we must stay with broad political issues and avoid concentrating on instances of atrocity. He quite possibly would object to the nonobjective, unpolitical, personalist treatment by St. Luke, say, of the crucifixion of Christ. On the other hand, it is perhaps not the ideal evangelical stance to take the long way round compassion in the name of political agreements arrived at by gentlemen of the cloth and gentlemen of the armed forces—each skilled in "reasoning together." This, while the stench of burned flesh permeates the air.

January 3rd. To Long Island to meet with youth groups on war, peace, civil rights. Another first! The exurban Catholic is actually more violent against Martin Luther King than he is against the peaceniks.

This was in truth a slum church. One had the sense, never felt in the ghetto, that here violence, alienation, and disgust for life were breeding. All the popular myths about the ghetto were fulfilled among the middle class. It was like a trip into wearying circles of hell. Clichés learned by rote, a kind of anti catechism-number-one. Low attention span to any new idea, rushing with refutations before one could finish a sentence. The sense here of the bitter truth that the sins of parents are being visited on children. The executive with liquor on his breath, anxious to prove that "King now has embraced violence."

The priest here has his suffering ready-made. And then I thought (and the thought was like gall in the mind): Is it for such a generation, already born with the itch for weapons, racist before it can know black from white, is it for such that we suffer as we do day after day in the hope of an hour which biology continually seems to make more distant? Again and again the young people leaped to their feet, filled with a hot sense of self-righteousness, of scraps and oddments of religion, bandaged in rags of justification like infected wounds that cannot be shown uncovered for very dread of healing. They are like their families, they are like their Church, they are like their President, they are like me. God help us.

5 / Litany
from the Underground, I

by ROBERT W. CASTLE, JR.

Leader: O God, the City, for people to live and work and to know one another,

Response: Help us to love the City

O God, the Metropolis, of all men's lives,

Help us to love the Metropolis.

O God, who lives in tenements, who goes to segregated schools, who is beaten in precincts, who is unemployed,

Help us to know you.

O God, who hangs on street corners, who tastes the grace of cheap wine and the sting of the needle,

Help us to know you.

O God, who can't write or read, who is on welfare, and who is treated like garbage,

Help us to know you.

O God, who lives and no one knows his name and who knows that he is nobody,

Help us to know you.

O God, whose name is spik, nigger, ginny, and kike,

    Help us to know you.

O God, who pays too much rent for a lousy apartment because he speaks Spanish,

    Help us to know you.

O God, who is uprooted by Urban Renewal to remove you from your neighborhood,

    Help us to know you.

O God, who is cold in the slums of winter, whose playmates are rats—four-legged ones who live with you and two-legged ones who imprison you,

    Help us to touch you.

O God, who is children in the grave, burned in the tenement fire,

    Help us to hear your cry.

O God, whose church down the street closed and moved away,

    Help us to touch you.

O God, who is old, and lives on fifty dollars a month, in one crummy room and can't get outside,

    Help us to see you.

O God, who is white and lives with Mr. Charlie, who is black and lives with Uncle Tom,

    Help us to see you.

O God, who lives in the projects of Federal, State, and City in indifference,

    Help us to see you.

O God, who is fifteen in the sixth grade,

    Help us to touch you.

O God, who is three and whose belly aches in hunger,

Help us to touch you.

O God, whose toys are broken bottles, tin cans, whose play-yard is garbage and debris, and whose playhouse is the floors of the condemned buildings,

Help us to touch you.

O God, who sleeps in bed with his four brothers and sisters, and who cries and no one hears him,

Help us to touch you.

O God, who has no place to sleep tonight except an abandoned car, some alley or deserted building,

Help us to touch you.

O God, who is uneducated, unskilled, unwanted, and unemployed,

Help us to know you.

O God, who was laid off last week and can't pay the rent or feed the kids,

Help us to be with you.

O God, who is a bum, a chiseler, who is lazy, because people say you are when you don't work and you want to work and you can't find a job,

Help us to be with you.

O God, who always gets the sweatshop jobs for a lousy buck and a quarter,

Help us to know you.

O God, all poor at welfare being told you don't want to work,

Help us to be with you.

O God, whose job at the factory is gone because the factory closed and left the city,

Help us to know you.

O God, whose union has a sweetheart contract with the employer and you get double-dealed every day.
   Help us to know you.
O God, who smells and has no place to bathe,
   Help us to be with you.
O God, who is dressed by the suburbs from the church clothing-store,
   Help us to touch you.
O God, who is chased by the cops, who sits in jail for seven months with no charges brought, waiting for the Grand Jury and with no money for bail,
   Help us to know you.
O God, whose blood is red, whose skin is black, whose red blood is on the billy club,
   Help us to touch you.
O God, who hustles fifty cents for lousy wine, who sells copper and lead to clean his cloths,
   Help us to touch you.
O God, who pushes a baby carriage at night to the cans of another's garbage and claims it as his treasure,
   Help us to know you.
O God, who works all day, who feeds and cares for her children at night and dreams of better days, and is alone,
   Help us to know you.
O God, who works all day for bare survival and is still poor and humiliated by landlord, employer, and government,
   Help us to know you.

O God, who is without power, voiceless, who has no share in his destiny,

> Help us to join you.

O God, who is unorganized, and without strength to change his world, his metropolis, his city, his neighborhood,

> Help us to join you.

O God, who is overwhelmed by the indifference, and apathy, and status quo of so many who are good Christians and in church on Sunday,

> Help us to join you.

O God, who is tired of his church and its ministers and priests, irrelevant and unbloody,

> Help us to join you.

O God, whose elected leaders only know you exist election time and represent themselves and not the people,

> Help us to touch you.

O God, whose local papers distort the truth, never listen to you, but represent the comfortable and powerful,

> Help us to hear you.

O God, who is poor and has all sorts of programs being planned for you, and people to speak for you out of both sides of their mouth,

> Help us to be with you.

O God, who is sold a bill of goods by phony white liberals,

> Help us to stand with you.

O God, whose enemy is white, powerful, and deaf, dumb, and blind,

Help us to stand with you.
O God, who is spoken for by black established-
leaders who the people do not know,

Help us to stand with you.
O God, who has leaders, black and white, who sell
you out,

Help us to be with you.
O God, who couldn't take it any longer and was
in the streets this summer, and was called a
hoodlum, communist, agitator, bum, wino, drug
addict,

Help us to know you.
O God, who carries a sign, sits on the ground,
strikes his rent, boycotts the store,

Help us to join you.
O God, who is fed up with it all and who is
determined to do something, who is organizing
people for power to change the world,

Help us to join you.
O God, who has had it and dreams of a new day
and is on the march across the land that he might
make his own destiny,

Help us to join you.
O God, who is black and who is white and who
would change the world for peace, justice, truth,
and love,

Let us organize together.
O God, who is black and who is organizing for
his own black power,

Help us to support you.
O God, who still is,

     Help us to be.
O God, who is full of guts to be,
     Help us to join you.
O God, who is all men joined together in all peace,
all truth, all justice, all love,
     Help us to love you.
O God, the City,
     We need you.
O God, the City,
     We need you.
O God, the Holy City,
     We love you.

6/ The Church and Civil Rights

by *JAMES E. GROPPI*

When I am helping the Milwaukee N.A.A.C.P. Youth Council in a civil rights action, the phone rings often with requests from people who want me to come on a sick call. When a secretary tells the caller that she will obtain another priest and tries to get a name and address, the indignant retort is, "You mean a dying person cannot see this priest? What did he become a priest for? Why doesn't he stay where he belongs?"

This bespeaks a common mentality found in the Church today. It sees the role of clergyman and Church as involved solely with the life hereafter. It dichotomizes religion, dichotomizes man. Here is the temporal order; there, the supernatural. The Church is narrowly to confine itself to the supernatural realm and close its eyes to the needs of suffering humanity. The Christian, in patterning his life in a similarly blind fashion, is to go to church each Sunday and conform to Church legalisms.

Quite to the contrary was the gospel preached by Jesus Christ. Christ never preached noninvolvement. The Gospels celebrate the good news of Christ's concern for suffering humanity. His concern was such that he fed the hungry—the story of the loaves and fishes. His concern was such that he cured the sick and the lame and made the blind man see.

Because of his concern for the loneliness of the widow, he raised her son back to life.

Instead of spreading this good Word, we have reduced it to a list of do's and dont's; we have stripped it of its life-giving power. To institute means to get going, but we institutionalize to the point of death. So close do we come to suffocation that the instinct of self-preservation takes over. We think only of more members, more funds—keep the institution going. We tend to forget the original purpose of the institution. The Church is to be the sign of Christ present in the world today, but our sign has become incredible. The Church, therefore, must refind and renew this very Christian and human concern for suffering humanity, for the needs of one's neighbor. The Church must constantly be putting into central focus the teaching of brotherhood, which, as Gandhi has said, is common to all religions.

The very title under which I am writing, "The Church and Civil Rights," is comprehensible to our compartmentalized mentality only as a violation of the separation of Church and state. Yet once we have really accepted the radical notion that God is the Father of us all, then we see our fellowman, not as part body and part spirit, but as a brother from whom we will not be separated, especially if he is in need. And we see the injustice of festering a brother's wounds by telling him that he will be rewarded in another life. Distinctions raised by anyone which would effect a separation between us who are one family are as irrelevant as knowing the number of angels able to dance on a pinhead.

Rather, if the Church is to be at all relevant to the needs of suffering people, the cancer of racism which quarantines brother from brother must be wiped out. What we need to accomplish this renewal of Church and society are men of courage.

In city after city throughout this nation the issue of open housing is pressingly real. The mayors of these cities realize they have a moral hot potato in their hands. They consistently refuse to handle it; they try to throw it into the hands of the state, of the country, or of the people. They propose a referendum on the issue, a referendum which concerned people know cannot be won because of the number of bigots in our cities. Are not such actions akin to those of Pontius Pilate? Pontius Pilate had Christ before him and knew he was innocent. But because he was afraid, he washed his hands and said, "I am innocent of the blood of this man. The responsibility is yours." Is not this exactly what the city leaders did in fearing to commit themselves?

All too often, too, the Church leaders have played the same role. We rationalize and politick, afraid to put ourselves completely on the line for what is right. We see evidence of the lack of commitment in regard to this matter of open housing. Although in 1966, the Bishops' Conference in Washington issued a statement pointing out the need for open housing and for the preparation and education of the White community for open housing, they did not outline a program of implementation. Official reaction in Milwaukee virtually negated the value of even such a statement by saying that this was putting the cart before the horse. The real problem was said to be employment. Yet the high rate of Negro unemployment and the frequency of job discrimination against Black men has yet to be deplored by Church officials. The same is true of the third-rate schools found in the inner core. Nor have Catholic schools been integrated. In fact, we cannot even get a sermon outline on interracial justice.

To dichotomize the spiritual and temporal orders to maintain the old attitude of isolationism through preaching is in reality a betrayal of the teachings of Jesus Christ. Our words are hollow if we preach about man's obligation to God without underscoring man's responsibility to make God's presence visible in this world. Conforming to Church legalisms are meaningless if we are at odds with our brother. "If your brother has any grievance against you, leave your gift at the altar and go and make up with your brother; then come back and present your gift." It is amazing how we have fallen away from the teaching of Jesus Christ.

I recall an ex-marine coming to the Youth Council. This young Black man had been three and one half years in the marine corps, six months of which he spent fighting in Vietnam. When he came home, the young man and his wife sought a dwelling just two blocks beyond the ghetto area. The landlady, a gentle elderly woman, hesitated before telling them that she had already rented the place. The young man's wife confronted the owner, asking, "It's because we're Negro that you won't rent to us, isn't it?" The landlady tried excusing herself in her reply. "Well, I can't rent to you. What would the people downstairs think? What will the neighbors say?"

This was during the Advent season. I could not help but think that this elderly woman had probably gone to church each Sunday of her life. And probably every Christmas, she had heard about Mary and Joseph and how there was no room for them in the inn. Perhaps she had even wept over their plight—snow falling, Mary pregnant, and no room in the inn. Yet religion had become so irrelevant to her that in the face of the young man at her own door she did not see the face of Joseph. In the face of his wife she could not see the face of Mary. It is in just such situations that Christianity is at its test. Either the Church becomes involved completely in the struggle for social justice, or the Church should close its doors because it has become like the Scribes and Pharisees whom Christ condemned, a whitened sepulchre.

The Reverend Jesse Jackson of the Southern Christian Leadership Conference has appropriately termed this "ecclesiastical gymnastics." Many of us get involved in the performance of certain liturgical functions as ends in themselves and thus never use them as a means of bringing the real message of Christ to the world. We must preach the Christian message of brotherhood and equality, and today in America with specific regard to racism; we must kill this evil in our society. We must constantly grow in our relationship to our brother.

There are those Christians who agree that racism is a moral evil but advocate prudence in removing it from society. They fear losing people as Church members; they fear losing money. If preaching the message of justice and brotherhood and the condemnation of racism means that half of our congregations are going to stop coming to church on Sunday, we will lose millions of dollars. But perhaps the Church has to die, perhaps it has to be crucified, in order to experience resurrection.

The members of the Milwaukee Youth Council have been a source of inspiration to me because of their courage, because they are "shock troops" in the cause of love and justice. They always take the lead. During the early days of our open-housing demonstrations they were literally almost killed. We have all been in jail; we have all eaten tear gas. As the demonstrations progressed, as we were marching and singing together, we were growing in our relationship as brothers. White people and Black people were growing. In true intergroup relations, a person never ceases to grow. And the more we grow in brotherhood, the more we grow in the Spirit, for brotherhood and life in the Spirit, like the spiritual and temporal orders, are inseparable.

And this has ramifications in our concept of what constitutes morality. I believe that there is good and that there is bad. I do not believe that morality is synonymous with a negative attitude toward sex and abstinence from what we call bad language. Nor can what is moral be determined by what is socially acceptable, for society has set racist standards. Morality involves looking at what we are, children of God, and asking ourselves what strengths and what weaknesses we have contributed to the human family. I believe that all sin is social. Most basically, it is a separating of oneself from the family of men. When one sins, he must obtain forgiveness and do penance by repairing the break that he has in someway caused. Self-mortification, such as fasting, may have its purpose, but a family reunion is essential, for herein lies our salvation.

Racism has thoroughly pervaded the American system. I do not believe anyone has escaped its influence. The effect of our segregated society is that Black children grow up with an inferiority complex and White children acquire a superiority complex. I believe that one of the best ways of effecting brotherhood is through Black Power. Black Power removes the Black man from a position of begging for what is rightfully his to a position of demanding. Black Power teaches him to respect himself. Through the proper use of Black Power, the superiority complex in the White community can be cured because the White man will learn to respect the Black man. Respect always precedes love. When the White man learns to respect the Black man, he can learn to love him, not in a paternalistic or condescending way, but as an equal brother.

To begin this process of growth, a person must first honestly admit that he does not understand his brother completely, that he does not understand people of another culture or ethnic group completely. He must realize that he must learn, that he must grow in understanding and develop spiritually. Only then can he advance.

The Youth Council, for example, had sweatshirts made that

said, "Black and Beautiful." All people, Black and White,
must learn this. We have traditionally given the color black an
unfavorable connotation. We say blackball, black sheep,
blacklist, all in contrast to, at worst, little white lies. But there
is a tremendous white lie in this country, the lie that black is
bad. We must combat this lie with truth if there is to be growth
in the White community and in the Black community, growth
which will result in one community. Honesty is something that
we must all have if we are to be effective. We do not suddenly
reach a point where we can say, "I am not prejudiced." Our
attitude of mind must always be that I must grow in brotherhood and in understanding of my fellowman.

We must realize that racism permeates even our language.
This became obvious when several people came to purchase
sweatshirts and asked for one that said, "Black *but* Beautiful."
We must come to see that black is not bad, not something
beautiful in spite of being black. Black *is* beautiful and good.

All should have, and indeed all do have, a responsibility to
become involved in the civil rights struggle. If we really believe in brotherhood, Whites as well as Blacks must be involved completely in some aspect of the struggle for equality.
Unless a man is involved in this struggle, he becomes increasingly less and less human. It is a moral issue, a struggle between right and wrong, which concerns all mankind.

I cannot understand how a man who proclaims himself a
follower of Jesus Christ could think and act as a racist. Christ
worked with the poor, the Samaritans, the Publicans, the sinners, the afflicted, and all the others who were socially ostra-
cized. He understood their problems; he had compassion for
them in their suffering. He was crucified for his associations,
for his defense of the unacceptable. Yes, he admonished the
Samaritan woman at the well; but he did not call her "no
good." He certainly did not suggest in any way that the nature

of the woman's weakness had anything to do with the fact that she was a Samaritan. He never said that the Samaritan had to rise to a new height of morality before he could enjoy the right of freedom of association. In fact, Christ preferred the morality of the poor and of those relegated to a secondary status in society by reason of their ethnic origin. It was not the sins of the poor and the dispossessed and the unwanted that bothered him; rather, it was the hypocrisy of the Scribes and Pharisees that disturbed him. Christ's attitude toward Pharisaism was expressed in his words, directed to the Scribes and Pharisees, "whitened sepulchres." John the Baptist used even stronger words, "offspring of vipers."

How many Whites, calling themselves Christian, are indicted by these words of Christ and the Baptist? They are so indicted because they want Black people to be as moral as they consider themselves to be. I do not deny the presence of weaknesses in the Black family structure. But it has been White racist attitudes and actions that have helped to destroy the Black family. I agree with William Stringfellow that it is wrong to talk about the weaknesses of the Black family without at the same time talking about its inherent strengths and beauty. It is wrong to talk about the emasculation of the Black male without talking about the defeminization of the White female. I can never tell Black people to pattern their lives after a supposedly more moral White society. The conduct of White society in this country has hardly been Christian.

This is partially understandable when the men who assume the role of Christian leadership themselves distort the teachings of the Jew from Nazareth, a distortion which stems as much from what they do not say and do as from what they do say and do—and when they do speak and do act, often such speech and action reflects only a partial commitment to Christian love and justice. Truly concerned clergymen do not waste their time, while sipping tea or martinis, gossiping about the personal problems of their parishioners. Unfortunately, the members of clerical sewing circles have little, if any, understanding of and empathy with the Black man in White America. They may talk about love or justice in their pulpits, but in practice they accept the racist ethos of the White power structure.

I have been in the past, and still am, critical of Church leadership in its lack of commitment to the Black man's struggle for equality. We have neglected our job of bringing Christ's word of justice and brotherhood to society today. I have been in the South and have seen there the lack of commitment of the Church on the part of many individuals. The excuse of Catholics down there was, "We really can't do much because we are only three percent of the population." My answer was simply, "Well, then, what have you got to lose?" A Benedictine priest, a Black man, told me a story of a group of sisters in Mississippi. He had asked them why they did not integrate their hospitals. They replied, "We can't, Father. The Ku Klux Klan sent us a letter saying that they would burn down the hospital if we tried to integrate." He answered, "That would be wonderful. You would all be martyrs for the cause of social justice and the brotherhood of man. For what better cause can a man die?"

It is only with caution that I speak of the South. Too often people have excused their own lack of concern for their neighbor by pointing at the South and calling this a Southern problem. Having worked primarily in the North, however, I can see the truth of the statement of Malcolm X—there is only one South in the United States; it is everything south of the Canadian border!

When Black people began to move in large numbers to Milwaukee's Near-North-Side, Whites fled to the suburbs. My own parish, St. Boniface, was once considered a flourishing Catholic parish of more than a thousand families. Yet these good Christian families who filled the church Sunday after Sunday sold their homes in panic when Black people rented next door or down the block. It makes one wonder what kind of religion was taught when there existed this complete lack of understanding of human and Christian brotherhood. The Milwaukee Archdiocese closed two of its churches in the inner core and moved one of these parishes to the suburbs. There were thousands of Black families in these neighborhoods— people who were hungry, people who needed clothes, people who needed jobs. But not enough of them were Catholic, so we closed our eyes to the needs of our Black brothers. Priests in the inner core were becoming fewer and fewer, and too few understood Black beauty and Black culture. When I was assigned to St. Boniface, I was told to work on getting converts. The irony of this struck me with its full force during a school boycott. We were forbidden to use our parish facilities for freedom schools. Hundreds of Black children were waiting on the steps to attend what they thought would be a freedom school. So I had to lead almost a thousand children to a Baptist church two blocks away. Forget about a third-rate school system; increase the number of Catholics! But we can no longer sit in comfortable rectories and ignore suffering people. And that today we have several more priests assigned to work in the core of the city and assigned on the basis of interest is due, I believe, only to pressure and the focus of attention on problems such as I have been discussing here.

About twelve years ago I met a woman living in unbelievable poverty. She was living in the vicinity of what had once been St. Joseph's parish. The church had been torn down to make way for an expressway, and because of the exodus of the Whites to the so-called "better" sections of the city and to the suburbs, the church had been rebuilt in an affluent White neighborhood. There were more Catholics there than in the Black ghetto where the church had once stood, and this provided the rationale for not rebuilding the church in its original parochial area.

This woman, who had come from Mississippi, had five children. She had never learned to read and write because the White man in the South had told her she had no time for those things. All her life she had been called a "nigger." Early in life she had been taught that her proper function in life was to pick the White man's cotton and to satisfy his lust. So, she came to Milwaukee looking for a better life.

The people in the normal White parish do not know hunger; they do not fear that their children will be bitten by rats as they sleep on filthy mattresses at night in a hot stinking room. But she and her children knew what it was to be hungry, what it was to live with the presence of rats, what it was to breathe the stench of a deteriorating slum building.

She could not get any welfare money because she had not been in Milwaukee for a year. And what employer is going to hire a Black woman from Mississippi who cannot read or write? Finally, she found a job, picking chicken feathers for less than fifty cents an hour. But she got tired of begging to supplement her inadequate wages in order to feed her children. Yes, you guessed it. She became a so-called prostitute. She sold her body at night in order to feed her children the next day. The tragedy is not her prostitution but the judgment of White Christians who call her an adulteress. This reminds me of one of the Gospel incidents: the weeping woman crouching at the feet of Jesus, waiting to be condemned by him as she had been by the Pharisees. Listen to his words: "Let him who is without sin among you cast the first stone."

How many White Christians have had the audacity to throw the first stone?

A kind of creative tension, such as that generated by the Milwaukee Youth Council, must continue if our society is to renew itself, if the Church is to become relevant and measure up to Christ's teachings of brotherhood and justice. How far we have to go was apparent one day as I took several Youth Council members to look for a new headquarters. We had been discussing the need to have a place of our own, one large enough for meetings and rallies, along with office space in order that we might keep some records and answer our mail. We saw a place which would answer these needs. It stands there, a monstrous old Gothic church. Surrounding it are housing projects, alive with people, filled to capacity. The church and surrounding yard were spooky in their emptiness. With spires reaching toward the sky, here, physically symbolized, is dramatized the irrelevance of the Church.

During the Youth Council's demonstrations for open housing we have been criticized for our use of the church for what we call prayer gatherings or, in other terminology, freedom rallies. Here one is looking at the church-building from two different viewpoints. The criticism is generated by a culture which views the parish church as a place where one goes and remains in perfect silence, a place to contemplate a life after this one. In my own impression, this concept of the church-building removes the Church from this world; it is more or less shut down, like a vacant building, and plays little part in people's lives. In contrast is the idea of the Church as viewed from a Black cultural background. A member of the Youth Council expressed this to me one evening at a rally. He said, "This to me is what the Church should be. It is a place where people of different races and different religions gather together in prayer, sing hymns, talk about our problems, the problems of suffering humanity. Then, from this gathering, as the people of God, we go forth and do something about suffering humanity."

In the Black community, the church-building has always been used for this purpose. A great many, though not all churches, were just such gathering places. People came together, talked over problems, and attempted to do something about them. Today when we demonstrate we preach a sermon, and the sermon is that there are inequities existing in society. When we protest, we are preaching justice. When we sing openly and loudly in church, when we discuss issues existent in society, we are praying because we are making religion relevant.

The teaching of Jesus Christ is the teaching of brotherhood and justice. This must be the role of the clergyman. When there are injustices existing in society, the Church has a moral responsibility to become involved in whatever way necessary to bring about social change. If there is a violation of the social teaching of the Church in the political and the temporal order, the Church must be involved in doing whatever it can. Many clergymen, concerned about suffering humanity, have been and are involved. Many are not. I do not believe we can issue a blanket indictment of the entire Church. I will always be critical of the Church, however, until it becomes, as one member of the Youth Council put it, what it is supposed to be—the most radical civil rights group in this country. Brotherhood is essential to religion. There is nothing which attacks the teachings of Christ, or the synagogue, more than the disease of racism. We must root out the cancer of racism completely. We must follow the most radical civil rights leader who has ever lived.

No civil rights leader in the history of this country was ever nailed to a cross because of his belief in social justice and the brotherhood of man. Christ was a revolutionary. The peace he preached was that of inner conviction and human dignity. He never meant that creative tension should be removed from this world. There is only one way that a man can find life after death and that is through involvement in this life—through a deep, sensitive concern about the sufferings of people, a concern which leads to action. To keep the faith is to keep trying to unite men in a society of brotherhood. This is the role of the Church.

7 / Black Power vis-à-vis "The Kingdom of God"

by *JAMES E. P. WOODRUFF*

For six years I have been a denominational chaplain at three "Negro" institutions of higher education. These institutions would fondly prefer to be called "predominantly Negro," but they are in fact "Negro" schools. During most of their histories they have had integrated faculties and administrations. Fisk has exchange students that come from Maine, California, Iowa; in fact they come from all over. But they are all white. It does not have exchange programs with "Negro" schools.

At this point it will be helpful to indicate that the word "Negro" will be used in a very specific way. Largely because of the influence of Black Muslim teachings about this word, especially as propounded by Malcolm X, many people in this country have become aware of the many negative connotations surrounding the word.

To help explain how the word "Negro" will be used, let me begin by recalling the words of Muhammed Ali who explains that Chinese come from China, Irish come from Ireland, Italians come from Italy, Germans come from Germany; but where is Negroland?

This was a name given to a race of people, who, unlike the other racial and ethnic groups in this country, did not choose to immigrate to the United States and the rest of this hemisphere. Rather, the African was brought here against his will and was relegated to a disgraceful lot as a slave. In order to keep the enslaved African from rebelling more than he did, the slavemaster realized the importance of attempting to mentally enslave the African.

The program of "nigger-making," to borrow a phrase from a great Black author, was begun. The African was carefully separated from his countrymen so that people who shared specific cultures were moved far apart. This, of course, meant that their cultural patterns of religion, language, and nationalism were virtually destroyed. It is difficult to overthrow an oppressor, when the potential revolutionaries cannot share ideas and plans.

Not only could the African slaves not communicate with each other from the depth of their cultural patterns, but they also could not meet. The right of freedom of assembly was denied them as vigorously as it was fought for by the European-Americans. This led to the development of the Spirituals, which were used as parts of carefully contrived codes. For example, they announced secret meetings by such a Spiritual as "Steal Away." Even so, the slaves were under constant surveillance, and whenever the slaves would begin to get together, they were either killed or sold to a faraway owner.

The slaves fought bitterly in their own ways, such as by poisoning the slavemasters, setting fires to homes, ruining crops, and constantly trying to escape. However, the greatest fight of all took place in their hearts. They sustained segments of their culture through rhythm and gesture. They ridiculed their white masters' hypocritical Christianity by using Spirituals, such as "Swing Low Sweet Chariot." The complacent slave owner fantasized that his slaves were satisfied to work for him and were content to be carried to "Heaven" by an ignominious band of angels. The slavemaster would have been shocked out of his fantasy if he had realized that home for these proud Africans was across the Atlantic, and not in a white Heaven where, were it left up to their slavemasters' God, they would have been slaves again. They longed for their deep culture, for their society of values that for the large part had been practiced, not merely preached.

The slavemasters' paranoia was, in fact, reality. Deep in the hearts of the millions of oppressed Africans, who were relegated to an incredibly beastly existence, there was an insatiable thirst for freedom. The slavemasters' nightmarish visions of these proud Black men rising up in the night to free themselves, by any means available, were for the slaves the lifeblood that ran through their souls, enabling them to go on. The slaves never gave up the hope of escaping.

When the Civil War finally came and went, the newly freed slave was psychologically a bastard in the American scheme. His roots had been disgracefully severed, and the ex-slave African had nowhere to turn in order to regain his identity. Before the Civil War, efforts were made by people like William Lloyd Garrison to teach the African in America to be a "Negro." Unfortunately, many people admired the work of the white abolitionists, but there were some who recognized white supremacy regardless of which guise it wore. Basically, most abolitionists wanted the slave free in order to be returned to Africa or, more specifically, to Liberia. The essence of their beliefs is summed up in the words of the "Great Emancipator":

And, why should the people of your race be colonized and where? Why should they leave this country? You and we are different races. We have between us a broader difference than exists between almost any other two races. Whether it is right or wrong I need not discuss, but this physical difference is a great disadvantage to us both, as I think. Your race suffer very greatly, many of them, by living among us, while ours suffer from your presence. In a word we suffer on each side. If this is admitted, it affords a reason why we should be separated.

Another example of this idea is found in Governor Hunt's annual speech to the New York Legislature in 1852. He suggested that money be appropriated to help send the free Blacks to Liberia. In response to this the free Black community in New York said at the New York State Convention of Colored Citizens in 1852:

And lastly . . . we protest against this appropriation, because "we remember those that are in bonds as bound with them"; bone of our bone and flesh of our flesh, may evil betide us when the hope of gain, or the fear of oppression, shall compel or persuade us to forsake them to the rayless gloom of perpetual slavery.[1]

The then technically free African in this country began a new phase in his history in America. It was clear that he was not going to leave the country, into whose soil the blood, sweat, and tears of the African had been poured. The contribution of the slave toward the prospering young country had made him a valuable stockholder in its economy. The Afro-American began to climb the long and dangerous road toward collecting his dividends.

Many solutions were put forward. Black Revolutionary Nationalism fostered the idea that the Afro-American should take land that he had more than earned. Another idea was Black Zionism which, in essence, suggested that the Afro-American ought to leave America because it was an evil coun-

[1] *The Liberator,* March 5, 1852.

try and that its evil values contaminated the proud history of a great people.

These ideas, however, never reached the masses of the newly freed slaves. In fact, no tangible program of rehabilitation has ever reached the masses of the field-slaves who were technically set free.

The only program that did filter down to a small number of house-slaves was that which was started by a few white Christians with "missionary syndrones." Their basic thesis was that the problem of the newly freed slave was his lack of education; they believed that if the newly freed slave could be educated, then he could eventually fit into the mainstream of American life. Therefore, they began programs of education. One of the first schools to emerge from this movement was Fisk University. (Fisk is one of the schools I serve.) These schools were largely financed by fathers of the bastard mulattoes who comprised their early student bodies.

When one looks carefully at these schools, it becomes clear that the so-called values that they attempted to teach are rooted in the heritage of white culture. Although there were certain traditions that might be called "Negro," their basic thrust was toward making a citizen that would be able to *conform* to the already existing white culture. It is shocking that, on the whole, "Negro" universities have very weak, or nonexistent, "Negro" history courses, "Negro" music courses, African language courses, "Negro" literature departments. (They have faculty members whose monumental publications are not available in their libraries nor sold in their bookstores.)

To make this absolutely clear, the teaching of white culture in itself is not the problem. However, to teach the culture of one people to another cultural group, to the exclusion of their own culture, is absurd. When everything that is anything is always about someone else, this whitewashing causes an insipid, unconscious masochism to permeate the psyche of persons taught in this way. It, simply stated, leads people under these circumstances to believe that there is nothing worthwhile that they are able to accomplish. Emulation, admiration, mimicking, and out-and-out copying then become the outward behavior pattern of these people. Self-denial, the denial of one's obvious reality, then becomes the internal behavior pattern. Psychologists agree that self-denial is one of the least effective of the defense mechanisms. It wastes psychic energy and produces a shallow person. Obviously, this pattern of identification is self-destroying and, therefore, immoral.

The futility and immorality of this pattern is not the whole story; it does not even make sense. One ponders how a people of one culture could turn around and in a dedicated manner eagerly accept the same oppressing culture. On the whole, the "Negro" university uncritically disseminates this evil culture at the expense of its own heritage. Not only is the practice futile and immoral, but it is also insane. These patterns have continued to the extent that many faculty members and administrators proudly brag concerning their efforts to build "Negro Harvards."

There have been voices of protest raised in the past, like those of W. E. B. DuBois at Fisk, Kwame Nkrumah at Howard, and Lewis Jones at Tuskegee Institute. Dr. DuBois finally left not only the "Negro" university but also the country and became an expatriate in Africa. Nkrumah returned to Africa, and Dr. Jones is still trying to awaken the "Negro" university to its responsibility to free the minds of Black people in this country.

Black Power challenges the educated "Negro" to meet this responsibility. The students at these universities, despite the efforts of these schools to stop them, have heard this call. They want *Black* universities. They are tired of being "Negroes" who display the patterns of self-denial as described before.

They have renounced lives of futility, immorality, and insanity. After the 300 years of "nigger-making," after the 100 years of "Negro"-making, the children of African ancestry have decided in favor of making themselves *Black* men.

They want to know their own heritage, both in this country and in the continent of their origin. They no longer believe Edgar Rice Burroughs' description of Africa. When Tarzan is attacked by a lion, the emerging Blacks cheer for the lion. They no longer believe that Gunga Din was a hero because he warned the British that his own great people of India were coming to take what was rightfully theirs. Quite the contrary; they see him for the low traitor that he was, and they cry out that he can keep the white heart that Kipling so "generously" bestowed upon him.

Thankfully, these are the changes that have taken place during my last six years in the "Negro" university. At this point, I would like to describe some of my experiences with the emerging Black men and Black women. Then, finally, I would like to make a Black theological analysis of these changes.

Six years ago marked the end of the first wave of nonviolent protest demonstrations: the sit-ins, the freedom rides, the wade-ins, and the look-ins—the "look-ins," because after the theaters, restaurants, motels, and hotels were "opened," the vast majority of Blacks in this country could only afford to look in. This tragic situation is the legacy of the integration movement.

The confrontation came when, after all this progress was made, it was clear that the vast majority of Blacks were not touched by these "steps forward." Unemployment in the Black communities continued; ghetto schools remained inferior; slum landlords continued their unholy exploitation; and rats continued to invade the cribs of the modern "slave" dwellings. The more important realization, after a few years of "progress," was that the basic causes of this pattern had not changed either. The same evil that enabled men to enslave others, the same pattern that allowed men to discriminate, debase, and deny fellow human beings their rights and privileges, was still the overwhelming reality exposed by the confrontation of the Sixties.

The leadership had proved to be irrelevant. The "Negro" leaders failed in their attempts to liberate their poeple. The old-line leadership had worked heroically to bring about civil rights for their people. They had the support, moral and financial, of many whites. These whites threw stones of criticism at the bigots without realizing that they themselves were to be proved as guilty in just a short time.

As Malcolm X points out, this was never an issue of civil rights but rather always one of human rights. The Civil Rights movement dealt with the symptoms of a sickness. In this case they were not the symptoms that the patient reported because the patient was never asked. Rather, these were the symptoms that the self-appointed doctors observed.

The courageous "Negro" students who bravely sat at the counters and rode the busses never consulted the patient either; because they were "Negroes," they had forgotten their own identification with the patient. They thought they had victory in sight. They would soon be graduated and would receive degrees. They thought that because they would be able to afford to attend movies, eat at fine restaurants, play golf, and participate in all of the leisurely activities that are built on the blood and sweat of underpaid degraded people in America and, indeed, in the world, they would have arrived. They failed to observe that the majority of these exploited people are non-white. Color instead of a lack of education remained the real problem.

The young Blacks asked the leaders: "Who are you leading? And toward what?" The "Negro" leaders replied they were preparing their people to enter the mainstream of American life. Maybe the Black man in this country was never close enough to the stream to smell the pollution. Whether he was close enough is not the question. The questions that were asked of the leaders were, How many got there? And where did they get to?

Who got there? In terms of the total numbers of Blacks in this country, the number that have entered the mainstream is negligible. It would follow, then, that if the vast majority do not move, the leadership has proved ineffectual. Meaningful perhaps, but, nevertheless, ineffectual.

The question, Toward what were Black people being led? required that the young Blacks begin to reexamine their presuppositions. Out of this exercise came the cry "Black Power." This phrase does not need to be defined; for Blacks it needs no explanation. Power means the ability to act, and on the whole, Blacks know that they have no power in this culture. The obvious answer to the question was that a move had to be made to enable Black people to have power.

A further examination of previous presuppositions demonstrated that some Black people did have power. Some had political power, some had financial power, and some had social power. But even that power was shaky. A Black doctor in Mississippi may have vast resources, but so that it will not be taken away, he must bow and scrape and camouflage this important fact of his life. There is no power if one cannot protect and use the advantages of his labor.

Then, like the dawn, it came. The overwhelming realization, again pointed out by Malcolm X, that Black people are persecuted for one reason. Black people are not persecuted because they are Methodists or because they live in the ghetto or because they are uneducated. They are persecuted because they are not *white*. They are persecuted because they are *Black*. Since the mainstream is the culture of the "nigger-maker," a theory of liberation that deals with individual Blacks moving into a mainstream would inevitably end with a *nigger-maker*-"Negro."

It then became absolutely clear that Black people had to change the system that made "niggers." It takes a great deal of power to nearly make a great people "niggers," and, therefore, it takes a great deal of power to end that machinery.

The Black community must liberate themselves, as a group, for themselves. It is simple! The "nigger-makers" must be disarmed by the Blacks so that every shadow of doubt might be removed. First and primary, the doubt must be removed from the minds of the Black people. Then the doubt that whites have will no longer negatively influence the lives of Blacks.

As students came under the influence of Black instructors, Black consciousness became a reality for them. Children of African descent were observed behaving as they had never behaved before. A certain young man from Trinidad began to say that no longer would a society of bigots define his manhood for him. He, together with thousands, under the influence of men like Malcolm X, began to shed off the psychological shackles that had imprisoned the minds and bodies of Black people for four hundred years.

Hungrily, these students began to seek self-identity. They began to discard the false divisions that had begun in the slave epoch and continued through the "Negro" epoch: divisions such as house-slave opposed to field-slave, light-skinned as opposed to dark-skinned, "good" hair as opposed to "bad" hair, big lips as opposed to thin lips—divisions that had pitted brother against brother. They accepted reality: no matter how much bleaching cream or hair straightening processes a Black person used, black skin was still black, and nappy, kinky hair was still nappy and kinky. And no matter what a "Negro" did, he was still a "nigger" and could not become white.

Once this inevitable reality was realized, the futility of the sinful escape as programmed by whites and "Negroes" could be abandoned. Black men and women began awakening to new dimensions of understanding. Almost suddenly, kinky hair was also beautiful, because Black people said so. Thick lips became beautiful, because Black people said so. The fact that Miss America contests display bad taste by promulgating only one standard of beauty became white peoples' problem. Obviously, if a person is able to recognize two or more standards of beauty, he then has more pleasant experiences than the person who can only see one. This rebirth was a broadening experience.

It had to broaden because it opened people to new and deeper understandings. It was an abandonment of an outmoded, decadent way of thinking and a returning to a "primitive" way, as it is called by white culture. The primitive biblical view of beauty is defined by the beautiful things a person does, not by how he incidentally looks. An ugly person is one who does ugly things. It is a tragedy when a woman has the beautiful stretch scars of childbirth on her abdomen and hides them because she feels they are ugly. It is tragic when a woman who dutifully allows a child to suck the milk of life out of her breasts, that were made for this reason, regrets the loss of her firm breasts. Firm breasts belong to a teen-age girl, not to a woman who has brought life to a child through her fantastic body. Men want women, not teen-age girls; perhaps "males" desire girls!

The understandings spread far beyond insights into mere physical appearance. Other new insights helped Black students realize why there are self-destructive patterns of living in this country. When self-destructive patterns are allowed to go unchecked and unchallenged, it is not surprising to observe people full of hate for themselves and everyone else.

They observed that these nihilistic patterns are not confined to the Black communities. For instance, they concluded that there is just as much illegitimacy in "respectable" society as there is in the Black community. After all, illegitimacy is in the relationship that conceives the fetus; the fetus is not illegitimate. A bastard is a victim of an illegitimate relationship. The monied community conceals their illegitimate relationships under the cloak of abortions and orphan homes or third and fourth marriages. A welfare mother cannot afford a divorce, so her children are dubbed "illegitimate."

That is just one of the unchallenged assumptions of "Negro" and white notions of respectability. There are hundreds more. To name a few, it is clear that most alcoholics are gainfully employed and live in nice respectable white and "Negro" homes. It is true that most of the trade of a whore comes from respectable white and "Negro" homes. It is true that some whites will keep their neighborhoods segregated and not forget to say grace. These notions themselves are the illegitimacy.

Now it is happening! The realization of the dream of the great Black leaders of the past. The young Black sees the "poor, lower-class" slum dweller as his brother. Perhaps this is why a Black college student, the son of a Negro doctor, can throw a brick at a cop in Nashville and Houston with the same facility as his brother who is a slum dweller in Harlem or Watts. The brotherhood of Blackness is synonymous in the American experience with the brotherhood of oppression. All oppressed people belong to that brotherhood. The brotherhood of Blackness then joins the American Black man with his oppressed brothers in China, Vietnam, Cuba, Bolivia, Algeria, Egypt, India, the Congo, South Africa, and with those few white Americans who, at last, are discovering the depth of their oppression.

If the brotherhood of the oppressed has anything of value, the supposedly superior "elite" will try, and indeed has tried, to take it by the "cheapest" means possible. It is interesting that for at least the past four hundred years this elite could be easily identified as the "brotherhood" of whiteness! To borrow a phrase from John Killens' *Freedom Century*, citizens have decided in favor of an overwhelming No to this exploitation. Maybe this is what Black college students mean when they triumphantly shout, "Hell no, we won't go!"

There was an interesting line from the movie version of "The Ugly American," when the Sarkahnese army officer reported to the American puppet and the American ambassador that his troops would not shoot their own people. If only American cops valued the lives of fellow Americans more than T.V. sets! The day is coming, and it is not far off, when it will come to pass that a white or "Negro" cop will not dare to aim a gun at a Black brother in the Black communities of this country! In fact, he may fear to bring a gun into the Black community if he dares to bring his body.

This is the consciousness that has led a Black student, who failed to graduate from a Negro University because she received a C-minus instead of a C from a white teacher, to exclaim, "It does not matter anyhow!" She was not rich and had had a hard four years. If her attitude is indicative of what many finishing college students are thinking, what about the attitudes of high school kids and drop-outs? Why have many of the dedicated workers of the Student Nonviolent Coordinating Committee, who hold major degrees, given up lucrative professions to earn possibly as much as $10 a week.

These are far-reaching questions to anyone who is concerned with humanity. Perhaps they are like the feelings that each parent of a male child must somehow deal with as he yearns to understand why his son must make war after thousands of years of "culture" and "civilization."

Let me conclude this by putting the situation in a Black theological perspective. A question that theological education spends a great deal of time dealing with is, What does Jesus mean by the kingdom of God?

Perhaps this question presents a problem because it is difficult for white and "Negro" middle-class men to place this important New Testament concept in the context of an existential perspective. While the world of Blackness is being robbed, raped, starved, and actually and potentially bombed to death, theological students ponder! They ponder saving a high-society marriage that never was a marriage. They ponder helping a criminal business man with his drinking problem by telling him he is understood by God, but never confronting him with his criminal practices. They comfort the slum landlord after his ulcer operation by talking about some foreign God's healing power, assuming this God is not at all opposed to his beastly existence.

We attempt to redeem the Sunday-School curriculum by looking for enriching curriculum material. When a new Roman Catholic catechism praises Dr. Martin Luther King, "faithful" Roman Catholics object, labeling it "socialist" and "leftist," and they object because King is not a "Catholic." Ecumenically we try to end denominationalism, when these denominations had little to do with the struggle of good against evil in the first place.

Our concept of ecumenism must go far beyond the borders

of the already existing sterile sanctuaries of segregation and obsoletism. It might be scandalizing for a churchman to realize that a person who publicly denounces the Christian faith might have more in common with Jesus Christ than the most faithful churchgoing, tithing hypocrite that dons the cloak of piety, while he readily hates "niggers" and the Vietcong. The disciples of Jesus were equally scandalized when the astonished Jesus told them that he had seen more faith displayed by an enemy, a Roman Centurion, than he had seen in all of Israel. This Centurion had placed himself in an extremely embarrassing situation because he was concerned for the health of one of his servants.[2]

It is clear that as a result of the confrontation of the Sixties the Christian Church, as it presently exists, is in serious difficulty. A community of Christians, who by definition are supposed to be committed to the eradication of injustice and evil, is by no stretch of the imagination even in the arena of the struggle. Not only is that true, but it is also ironically clear that some of the most active perpetrators of the injustice and evil in our culture hold high places in the ranks of the Christian Community.

The confrontation has forced some within the ranks of the established Christian Community to ask whether the Church can afford to be the defender of the segregating, offensive status quo. Can Christians defend notions such as respectability and The American Way of Life? Respectability has meant that a person could "achieve" by any means as long as he did not get caught. It has even meant that one of the obvious structures of respectability is keeping a "nigger" in his place. The American Way of Life is so full of a history of robbery, murder, rape, and exploitation that it is incredible that any-

[2] Cf. J. B. Phillips translation, Matt. 8:10.

one, especially a Christian, could even begin to think about being proud of this way of life.

A simple reading of any of the Gospels indicates that Jesus and his disciples were in direct conflict with the status quo, the respectable society. He was assaulted by the high priests, the magistrates, and the molders of public opinion, the Pharisees. These were the people who had established oppressive patterns against many people of their time. It was against these injustices that the power of the kingdom of God was manifested. God, through Jesus, did not give his power so that individuals could build church buildings, or have chauffeur-driven bishops, or carpeted offices. God's power, through his Word, was promised to those who made uncompromising commitments against evil practices inflicted on the oppressed people of Israel. If a person reading the Gospels does not clearly see this, then it is obvious that this person is not able to read.

It has been suggested that the authentic role of the believers in Jesus Christ is to be the bearers of the Word of God. When this Word is sounded, it exposes, confronts, and demands, at any cost, the righting of wrongs, the removal of injustice, the confession of sin, and the changing of evil self-destructive ways. There is indeed a profound promise given, but there is an expensive cost expected.

Compare the modern "monks" and "nuns" with the average, worship-service-attending, "believing" Christian today— with the comparison based on the criteria established by the words of Jesus Christ. The religious title of monks and nuns is a very appropriate synonym for the young Black activists in the university situation. Usually they are not concerned about marriage because their lives are in danger, and they know they will have no material security for sometime, if indeed ever. They more than likely will get "Red-listed." They own nothing and are not worried about it. They dress alike and wear similar hair styles. They very often live communal lives, sleeping on floors and eating very modestly.

At this point the analogy breaks down. Unlike the established Church's monks and nuns, these students are intimately involved with the poor and suffering people of their communities. They are not so bogged down with rules and regulations that they cannot move. They are selfless, in that they care about what happens to other people: this is the criterion for their success or failure. Like Jesus, the disciples, and St. Paul, they almost all have long prison records and have spent hours in the courts of this country. They are constantly misunderstood. They are condemned unjustly, and they utter no words of defense. They are compassionate and accept everyone where they are. There are no distinctions of class and breeding.

There is no need to articulate the description of the contemporary established Christian Community. It is altogether too familiar and clear to us all.

Is it the respectable churchman or the young Black activist who bears the marks of the Lord Jesus Christ?

The purpose of the Christian life is sanctification. The failure of the Christian Community is that it is uninvolved with suffering humanity. This uninvolvement leads to decay and sterility and a dedication to traditions. Worst of all, the Church is permeated with a morbid self-interested selfishness. These are symptoms of pathology. The Church is like "salt that has lost its savor."

The students who are freed from patterns of morbid self-denial and begin to have faith in their reality are different. They are enthusiastic (full of God). They are becoming everything that the Church claims it wants its people to be. They are dedicated, unselfish; they remember their conversions and, because they loathe their former beliefs, they are constantly thankful for their rebirth.

The Old Testament Jews renounced their covenantal oaths for the sake of their "unblemished" reputations. God decided to turn from them and to elect the Gentiles to be the bearers of his Word. Could it be that what "kingdom of God" meant to the Gentiles is what "Black Power" means to the Black Man?

8/ Church as Counter-sign: Process and Promise

by *MICHAEL F. GRODEN*
and *SISTER MIRIAM CLASBY, S.N.D. de Namur*

The informalities of preschool registration opened the way to conventional pleasantries about plans for community-center activities. But there was a tautness in the willowy beauty of the young mother and a growing brittleness in her voice as she chatted.

"Sure it's a good idea to have typing classes here, but there's no money for typists, even if you have the skills. Those man-power pools don't pay enough to live on. Last year I tried to make it holding down two jobs. This year I gave up the shoe factory and I take home $125 a week. I work as a barmaid. If that's what they want, that's what they'll get. . . ." Her tone held a final surge of desperation.

She was on the verge of unreachable hardness, and only a lived hope can confront such despair. At this moment it seemed that the neighborhood itself—her world—shared her sense of futility. The whole Highland Park section of Roxbury was a kind of void. There were many explanations for the rapid deterioration of the locale: the proximity of the ghetto, the new lower-income population, the outflow of white residents, the number of vacant and abandoned buildings. The closing of the private Catholic school in the center of the area

102

seemed to validate foreclosing on the neighborhood, to add one more reason for writing off its future.

Words alone could not change the situation. The blighted surroundings mirrored with searing accuracy the blighting of individual lives, the slow destruction of persons. The rich promise of the place was not being communicated to those living amidst its burdens of social and economic pressures. There was critical need for some manifestation of confidence in the latent possibilities and the neglected resources of the locale and its residents. There was an urgent need to redirect the momentum of change, to counteract the testimony of neglect by a reverse symbol, by a "counter-sign." Someone needed to express in unmistakable idiom, "It is good to be here."

The hunched concentration of the eleven teen-agers belied their apparent "cool" as they dissected their predicament. Dusty baseball awards and faded magazine photos—optimistic efforts at decor in the cellar clubroom—added a note of bravura to the intense atmosphere.

Wendell pinpointed the issue: "Those guys ruined our party by starting a fight. Do we go to get them?"

"If we do we might get creamed—and even if we don't, they'll be back after us."

"Yeah, and they probably won't be waiting with just sticks this time."

"Ya know, once it was fists—then kids got jackknives—then switchblades. Lotta guys got guns now. It keeps gettin' worse."

"An' ya never know when ya goin' ta get jumped. If you're with a gang it's not so bad. But some kid with a punk job figures he needs some of them silks and knits and takes ya for whatever ya have—even if it's only a buck."

"Okay. Let's vote. Start over there. Should we go after them?"

"I think we should. If we let those guys think they can get away with bustin' up the dance, they'll come to the next one to start somethin' again. We have to let them know we're tough, and they can't mess with us."

"Yeah, but you know what happens. We get them, then they keep tryin' to get us. . . ."

"Well, I don't really know. . . ."

Wendell seized the opening with a masterful stroke of diplomacy: "Okay, then. How many aren't really sure what we should do?"

Eleven hands shot up and they were "off the hook" this time.

The brief scene in the Hawthorne Youth Club demonstrated a basic philosophy of the place. The boys had gathered to talk about what was for them a crucial incident. The forum opened up for them some of the subtle dimensions of their predicament—the existence of the cycle of violence, the fact that it was getting worse, the sense that it was a trap. Confronting such basic problems of urban life, they were, in their own language, analyzing cause and effect quite incisively and correctly. They were growing in awareness and growing toward the next step—creative response. Even in describing their situation, they seemed to sense the futility of their world of weaponry, to recognize the possibility of alternatives. It would take a little longer for them to become aware that their joint efforts to understand could eventually refashion their lives and their community.

"What are they going to do to us?"

"They" referred indiscriminately to the urban renewal

authorities and their threateningly vague plans for Highland Park, to the trustees of the University of Massachusetts eyeing the section as the site for the fourteen-story towers of its urban campus, or to any of the nameless unmanageable forces that determine the future of the powerless.

The frantic urgency of the question arose from practical dilemmas. One twenty-five-year resident faced a basic decision: Should he sell or stay; should he invest in rehabilitating his house or add to the air of neglect by postponing work until plans for the future of the area were definite? His friend's predicament was more severe, but the man had withdrawn into inertness. Most of his earnings had been invested in yearly painting and improvements on his side of his duplex home. In the last five years the other side had changed hands ten times, from bank to bank, from tenant to tenant, until finally it had been condemned as uninhabitable. While most of his co-workers awaited retirement, he sat on his trim porch, waiting out the inexorable sentence which at some uncertain date would make the sole fruit of his working years irretrievably lost under the wrecking crane.

The question, "What are they going to do to us?" triggered plans for a lecture series in the summer of 1966 on "Community Renewal." Representatives from the Harvard-MIT Joint Center for Urban Studies and from the local Urban Planning Aid donated time and expertise to set up a seven-week program examining Highland Park, its history, its present condition, and its alternatives for renewal. Men from the Boston Redevelopment Authority, the Chancellor of the University of Massachusetts himself, and staff members from the Boston Housing Authority explored possibilities for the future with fifty or so residents who met each week.

According to the strategy, from these basic information-

sessions would emerge a group of citizens motivated to participate in planning the renewal of the area. The newly formed
Highland Park Council at first seemed the likely source for
organizing such involvement, but as weeks dragged into
months, it became apparent that the Council reflected conflict-
ing interests—those wishing to limit lower economic inflow
and those who felt it essential to provide low-rent housing.

To offset the foot-dragging of the official group, a half-
dozen residents who were convinced of the need for concrete
evidence of renovation incorporated privately to begin rehabilitating a prominent set of row houses on one of the central
streets. At the same time, the wheels for larger-scale opera-
tions were once more set in operation by contact with the city-
wide Model Cities Committee which offered new hope for developing the much-needed master plan.

Hawthorne House had provided the opportunity for members of the community to meet, to recognize a problem, and it
had collaborated in their effort to give shape to the future. The
Highland Park Council had proved an ineffective vehicle for
the undertaking. But it was quite in keeping with the rationale
that the initial plunge be rethought and reworked. Accommodation to existing realities constantly had to influence ultimate
direction and pattern.

The vast gray buildings that are now Hawthorne House
have deep roots in the past. As Holy Trinity School and Home
they had a long tradition of service to young and old alike.
The new venture underway is an effort to make a new kind of
Christian response. H. Richard Niebuhr calls "the pioneer
church" that part of society which, because it is most attentive
to the gospel message, is the most sensitive to the anguish of
the world and the most ready to respond. Hawthorne House is
an attempt to be present to a city with pressing needs. It is an

effort to listen, to sense the need, and to respond in a way appropriate for today. The cues that the city speaks today are unmistakable, and the incidents detailed above illustrate the problems of despair, violence, and powerlessness which demand confrontation. The young mother hardening in bitterness, the teen-agers moving towards insight, the adults grappling with bureaucratic circles and cycles—these are the people and the experiences determining the character of Hawthorne House.

When in 1966 the Archdiocese of Boston made the property and its four buildings available for community use, a nonprofit corporation was formed under the chairmanship of a young lawyer. Other local residents were elected to the Board of Trustees and a community-based, nondenominational educational operation was launched. Four religious congregations released members for the work: a Religious of Christian Education, a Sister of Charity of Nazareth, a Sister of St. Joseph, and a Sister of Notre Dame de Namur. Their presence signaled the Church as participating but not controlling. Along with two preschool teachers, they comprised the skeleton staff which, for the first six months, supported itself through private contributions. In January, 1967, an $18,000 Carnegie grant stabilized community-center activities until plans for multiple funding materialized.

In a locale where education had top priority among parents, precise programs evolved through interaction, consultation, and exploration with the parents. A timid summer day camp developed into a multi-faceted educational complex, housing an Office of Education curriculum resource center for Boston teachers and parents, a Manpower Training Program for health services, a training program for adult community leadership, as well as experimental preschool and elementary education. The Montessori-based preschool program began at once (with Headstart day-care services added later) as a logical base on which to build an elementary school. "Planning by doing" served as the operational philosophy.

Negotiations with the Division of Employment Security and the State Department of Vocational Education produced a broad-ranging training program for the health services with an innovative component for high school certification. Workers from local hospitals as well as administrators, university personnel, public school officials, and the state department staff— all contributed toward shaping the final plan. These groups produced circles of very different kinds of participants which defined the uniqueness of the planning pattern. These kinds of groups teach the Church that it must be part of, give to, and be enriched by the many circles of communities that constitute the workings of contemporary life.

The design resulting from this broad consultation does several things to the Hawthorne program. Working from the base of existing manpower programs, it reflects real community sensitivity by locating the program in Roxbury and by employing para-professionals from the area to recruit residents, especially those least likely to be reached by ordinary means. A parallel "Experimentation and Demonstration" component to redesign the basic courses injects a creative professionalism into the fairly rigid model of traditional manpower programs. The plan avoids older patterns of training which failed to provide built-in possibilities for advancement. By placing before the trainee a careful sequence of job development, it opens the way for a program developing from basic courses for a nurse's aide to such new ones as that for a medical assistant. A teacher-training process allows for the possibility that this year's trainee may be part of next year's training staff. By including among the consultants planners from the Boston school system, efforts to develop new curricula tie into the school system and provide a team of health professionals and a whole new design for vocational training in the health field which then can be adapted for the vocational institute being planned for the city.

For the moment, the final piece of the overall picture of Hawthorne House is a Community Service Training Seminary to prepare residents to serve on local planning groups and to operate a conference center. At this center suburban and urban residents, businessmen as well as teachers, can study urban development with residents who have firsthand experience in and information about problems of housing, education, and employment. The problem-solving seminars, again uniting urban specialists and local residents, will examine both theoretical and practical city issues. As with each other phase, the pattern represents an effort to provide the competence and confidence which is absolutely essential for a working "participatory democracy."

The multiplicity and variety of all these pieces may at first seem unwieldy, but there is an integrity which unifies. First priority is for innovativeness and quality of operation, with concern for the way in which such an operation can influence the structures of society educationally, politically, and socially. The second emphasis is on community participation, executed in such a way that residents are not just the products, but part of the process, of education.

What is emerging is a model urban education center. Its design encompasses all phases of education from preschool to adult retraining, each phase in its own way reflecting basic commitments to quality and to community development. Fundamental to all thinking is the principle of open-ended experimentalness. The proposed experimental school offers a paradigm for what can happen in administration and organization as well as in the curriculum. Concrete plans to involve staff and community in planning underline the conviction that on all levels there is need for a special sense of professionalism. Community representatives need to participate in significant ways in the educational process, to provide role-models for children, to demonstrate without words that education is important. Involvement of adults in an educational partnership implies a kind of reciprocity between parents and teachers, a mutual benefiting. Hopefully community members come to see themselves not merely as recipients and participants, but as people who help shape and refashion the process of education in this city and in others.

With this kind of community interaction with topflight educational innovators, the salient feature of the school should be the development of new types of relationships between community members and experts. Boston has some parent-run schools and some large-scale innovative school programs. The effort to blend them into a single structure ought to produce a *new* concept of the "neighborhood school."

The sweeping dimensions of the total vision of Hawthorne House are important, but even more important is the process of translating that vision into reality. The fluidity marking the operation frustrates every effort to capture the élan in a simple model or statement. Each piece belongs to the whole in a way which is intricate and yet fundamentally simple because of a basic integrating philosophy. The process of translation into specific activities depends on people with all types of experiences and disciplines coming together, understanding where they are, collaborating to creatively shape where they wish to go. The process must speak to the people of the city. It must be a process which speaks hope to those in despair, which offers opportunities to break the cycle of violence, which provides alternatives to the suffocation of powerlessness. The process itself is the "counter-sign," which even in meeting obstacles of postponement and failure spells out the possibilities of overcoming these obstacles and of living out a hope.

This process, through the weeks and months that we live it and live with it, provides, with its ups and downs, a reflective lens for a Church which cannot renew itself from within. Just as the Lord genuinely wept over the coming destruction of Jerusalem, although it would enable "his people" to break forth into a deeper catholicity, we must in this time courageously, even if sadly, abandon or reject, at times, encumbering traditional structures and expressions of Church life. The Lord's "people" must break forth anew according to his gospel message and his mandate to be a sign of hope and promise in the world.

The Greek Church adumbrated and exploited the mystery of Christ and of the promised sign of his abiding presence, the Church. The contemporary Church, too, when it recognizes, understands, and responds to the shapes and forms of contemporary life discloses some forgotten and lost richness in the meaning of Christ. But, even more, it reveals new themes of wisdom, hope, compassion, wholeness, and utility; new modes of activity as it struggles in continued fidelity to be the sign of what the Lord has done for all men. Never before could we see so poignantly the significance of the Church as "the minority serving the majority" (Congar), "the suffering servant" (Isaiah), "the unknown and uninvited fellow-traveller on the road to Emmaus" (Robinson), "diaspora" (Rahner)—a community knowing and celebrating the love and wisdom of Jesus, yet collaborating with every brother in the world that the Lord has made and remade.

Whole new things happen when we become flesh . . . when we come among our own . . . when we enter our own realm . . . when we are obedient to the incarnation of Jesus. This exposure energizes the Church; it catalyzes a new set of "tongues."

Hawthorne House is one attempt to sink sensitive and exposed roots into the realities of city life in such a way that the stock will bear the traits of fantastic strength needed to conquer in abounding hope the deadening feelings of desperation and despair. This is the *Underground* which supports working cells of local people creatively collaborating to bring to flower, through a sensitive, whole, and excellent educational environment, the inherent beauty of the youngster, the young adult, and the mature citizen. With such grounding, people bear fruit for their own continued development and for the human sustenance of their fellow city dwellers.

Since the day is gone when people have no alternative or power over the looming societal forces that form and deform human life, we need no longer be overwhelmed by life. We should, instead, be challenged by it, not simply because our age knows how to analyze its systems, to develop managerial competence, to coordinate expertise in aerospace technology, but because these developments allow us to appreciate the Creator's first command to fill the earth and *subdue* it. The Church, then, needs the world to recognize its purpose and its potentials.

Even though man may turn on his brother in envy, hate, and violence, if we will risk belief in Jesus, we can know that he has conquered the roots of sin and death and hate and hopelessness by emptying himself of power and becoming one of us. If we recognize that our power is from him, as he recognized his as his Father's, we will not be daunted by our experiences of evil, knowing that he has won the victory over every kind of death. We need only believe and help externalize in the lives of men their goodness, love, and beauty. Thus, our ecclesiology must reflect a creative and militant relationship with the world consistent with the creative expectancy of both old and new covenants. In striving toward the future we need no longer experience the world as an imposed fate or a sovereign, sacrosanct nature confining us. Rather it presents itself as a quarry, the raw material which we use to build a new world.

That Matthean account of the final judgment depicts the perennial reality that membership in the kingdom of the Lord hinges on what we *do* for our brother, not on what we do not do. Our age, however, has a different kind of hunger, needing a new food; a deeper kind of thirst, to be satiated by a stronger drink; a starker kind of loneliness, to be shattered by a different kind of loving; a nakedness, a sickness, and an imprisonment which do not lend themselves to easy or old answers. A handout at the door does more damage, perhaps, than good. Sympathy can be a mere palliative; individual kindness risks the danger of obscuring more fundamental responsibilities. The "doing" acceptable today is the basic alteration of the institutions, practices, and policies of society so that they reflect a more mature sense of justice. The "way of doing" must attest as well to a recognition of the fact that people are reached today far more decisively by relationship than by logic.

The gospel story of the talents is a two-edged sword. For Hawthorne House, it means utilizing all talents in terms of educational excellence to develop the abilities of each member of the community for his own sake and for the benefit of others. Thus, concern about the day-care service and efforts to insure employment progress for the mother through a training program in the health-service field are ways of saying in concrete terms, "There is hope that your life may be different." But it is also saying, "You are to make a contribution to the lives of others."

The "good news" about the freedom of the sons of God becomes perceptible and significant when its liberating message is specified as "counter-sign," as the possibility of escape from the cycle of violence enthralling teen-agers. It gives directives to them in their uncertainties, doubts, and unsureness ("How many aren't really sure what we should do?"). It makes it possible for them to think out together the factors and forces that constitute the cycle so that, understanding them, they may control and even break that cycle. The directives inherent in the life-death pattern of our liberating Lord indicate that only nonviolence can destroy violence and that we must choose to walk the second mile with the man who has forced us to walk the first. When the denigrating pressures forcing a man to gain through violence the symbols of respectability, stature, and status have been alleviated and are seen for what they are, these same teen-agers can come to see that it will be by their growing, their development, their doing for others, their freeing themselves, that they participate in making the world a more human community, and thus externalize the kingdom.

Hawthorne House is a nonprofit, nondenominational, community-based "thing," which might be called a "counter-sign" of hope and purpose and creative activity. It is not an ecclesiastical institution, its primary focus has nothing to do with a congregation. Yet it means the Church is present to this city today in a special way. And perhaps this is what the Lord intends in this age for his Church. Perhaps it is just to be the servant of the majority from a minority position, the unknown and uninvited fellow traveller on the road to the New City. This means that we rejoice to be his inadequate, unrecognized, even suffering servants, few enough to be a gathering, a community without a resting place who on occasion assemble, knowing and celebrating the love and wisdom of the Incarnate Word, collaborating with every brother to make a new worldly neighborhood.

9/ A Baptism Rite

by ANDY McGOWAN

In the name of the Father, of the Son, and of the Holy Spirit. Amen.

Let us recall the days when baptism began:

> In those days John the Baptist appeared, preaching in the wilderness of Judea. . . .[1]

> I am baptizing you with water, for your repentance. . . , he told the people, but one is to come after me who is mightier than I, so that I am not worthy even to carry his shoes for him. He will baptize you with the Holy Spirit and with fire. . . .[2]

> Then Jesus came from Galilee and stood before John at the Jordan, to be baptized by him. . . . It is I, said John, who ought to be baptized by you, and you come to me instead? Jesus answered: Let it be so for the present; it is well that we should thus fulfil all due observance.

This baptism rite was used in the christening of Mr. McGowan's son, Ian, on March 12, 1967, in New York City.

[1] Matt. 3:1. From the *New Testament* in the translation of Monsignor Ronald Knox, Copyright 1944, Sheed & Ward, Inc., New York. With the kind permission of His Eminence the Cardinal Archbishop of Westminster.

[2] Matt. 3:11.

John gave in to him and baptized him. As Jesus came out of the water, suddenly Heaven was opened and the Spirit of God came down like a dove and rested on Jesus. With that, a voice came from Heaven saying, "This is my Son, in whom I am well pleased."[3]

Let us pray:

Don't let this be simply a social occasion, Jesus. Touch the hearts of those present who associate Christianity only with superficiality and have become accustomed to religious exercises devoid of meaning.

Someone is being baptized into your own life and death. . . . Someone is being made a member of the church, of your own body. Don't let this baptism be shunted off into a . . . quiet hour with a handful of people. Let this baptism be a principal part of the whole church's life. . . . Make us all realize that we are profoundly involved in it because someone is being ordained to a lifetime of discipleship and ministry in your spirit and name. Amen.[4]

(The priest places his hand on head of the child.)

In your name, I lay my hand on your servant N—— and ask you to fill him with faith in you, hope in you, and love for you. Grant that he may walk in your commandments, and grant

[3] Matt. 3:13-17.

[4] "Prayer for a Baptism" from *Are You Running with Me, Jesus?* by Malcolm Boyd. Copyright © 1965 by Malcolm Boyd, p. 112. Reprinted by permission of Holt, Rinehart, and Winston, Inc.

him the wisdom, courage, and freedom to know your will and follow it.

We welcome him into the world and into the brotherhood of mankind. Unite him with the people and institutions that fulfill your will; unite his conscience with your will and make him the servant of his conscience. Let him put these things before membership in a tangible church.

(*The priest removes hand from child's head.*)

Further prepare him for his journey by giving him the power to recognize and control in himself the devils that are in all men:

—the one that makes us turn advantage to arrogance— let him respect as equals and show concern for those less secure or with less material, social or political standing;

—the one that makes us put "our own" before others— let him not put his self, family, associations, or country before others in a selfish manner;

—the one that makes us forget the dignity of those with whom we disagree—let him distinguish between ideas and those who espouse them; love and respect will make dialogue easier;

—the one that makes us fear and resist needed change— let him judge ideas on their merit, without prejudice.

Also, if he carries any stain inherited from the origins of mankind, let it be washed away.

(The priest stands over the water, the garment, and the candle to bless them. He may make the sign of the cross over them.)

Now, Lord, bless the symbols we use to effect this baptism:

—bless the *water,* which will purify and strengthen him;

—bless the *garment,* which he will wear as a visible sign of today's blessing;

—bless the *candle,* which he will receive to light his way. (Priest lights candle.)

(The parents or the sponsors hold the child over font. The priest applies the water, saying:)

The Servant of God N—— is baptized in the Name of the Father, of the Son, and of the Holy Spirit.

(The parents or the sponsors put the garment on the child.)

(If there are sponsors, the priest says:)

N—— and N——, as you dress N—— in the baptismal garment, treat the act as a pledge to see that today's blessing is fulfilled.

You represent the world in which N—— must make his journey. Be an example to those who influence him and can affect his freedom to follow his conscience.

(The priest says to the parents or the sponsors:)

Take this candle for N___. May it illuminate in proper perspective the true nature of all people and things as measured in the light of God, and leave in shadow false and distracting appearances, like false claims of purpose and people's superficial identities.

Go in peace.

10/ Up from the Underground

by GEORGE J. HAFNER

The spin-off from Vatican II's *Dogmatic Constitution on the Church,* instead of gently sweeping cobwebs from the corners of the ancient Church, has produced a veritable hurricane which threatens to bring the whole structure crashing down. One of the principal effects of this document was the formation of the conviction in Catholic laymen that the Church must no longer be described in terms of a hierarchical, monarchical society, but rather as a brotherhood of believers sharing the Spirit of Jesus. The division between the hierarchy and the clergy and between the clergy and the laity has come to be recognized as a distinction based on different kinds of service within the Church rather than on higher and lower degrees of participation in Church life. The tight ship guaranteed by the concept of a divinely-guided hierarchy and a submissive laity is beginning to feel the stirrings of mutiny. Reactions to arbitrary decisions by the hierarchy range from secret disobedience to open uprisings. The open protests in favor of Fathers Berrigan and Curran and the formation of the National Association of Laymen were almost without precedent in the American Church. The hierarchy's tolerance of these situations set the stage for a general demand by the nonhierarchical Church for equal partnership in the decision-making department of the Church. Fifteen years ago such an idea would have been considered heretical.

One of the most intriguing forms of mutiny, however, is to be seen (or rather, not seen) in the Underground Church. Everywhere in the United States, and reportedly throughout the world, people have begun to implement Vatican II in direct opposition to the controls imposed by the hierarchy. Small groups of laity with the help of priests who are willing to risk penalties are gathering together to search for the meaning of the gospel of Jesus in their lives. This they do in a liturgical experience which corresponds to real life. The performance of a mechanical ritual out of the past has become more and more intolerable for thinking Catholics. The implications of this kind of "bootleg" liturgy are not even completely understood by the participants. It was only after the formation of an "Aboveground" Church by the author of this article that the full implications began to make themselves felt.

The very fact that the formation of an unauthorized experimental parish by a group of twenty people became an incident of national importance and that it was immediately threatened with the ultimate ecclesiastical weapon (excommunication) gives clear indication that something more is at stake than control of the rubrics. In these pages we shall try to examine some of the theological problems created by the Underground Church.

Authority. Perhaps the most crucial issue, from an institutional point of view, raised by the Underground Church is the question of hierarchical control of Church life. The interventions of Paul VI to change the wording of some Council decrees at the end of the third session of Vatican II provoked an outcry which was the signal announcing the demise of the monarchical Church. Rumblings in the aula and coalitions to protest the Pope's interference, as well as cries of outrage from the secular and religious press, should have convinced a serious observer that the old system of unquestioning obedience to the Roman pontiff was in for a rude testing. And if the pope's powers were subject to question, what could the local bishop expect with his less clearly-defined magisterial rights?

The age of effective monarchies is long over. Totalitarian rule is frowned upon throughout the Christian world. Yet the Church continues to demand of men, whose whole style of life is democratic, blind submission to a human authority as coming from God. The medieval theory of the divine right of kings has been completely abandoned by secularized society, yet the Church continues to propose it to its adherents. The standard Catholic theology of obedience still pretends that the will of Church authorities manifests the "will of God." The hierarchy are said to be "divinely appointed" and "divinely guided". Not only does the hierarchy's claim to know the "will of God" smack of predestination, but the whole claim of divine appointment and divine guidance is unbelievably naive in the modern world.

Until recently it seemed perfectly acceptable to almost all Catholics that the pope and the bishops should be free to rule The Church without criticism since they were "divinely appointed." The recent exposure of the system of Church politics and a more honest reading of Church history have made it impossible to demand faith in divine appointment except from among the most unsophisticated. With an awareness of the selection-procedure for bishops it seems completely dishonest to modern secularized man to pretend that his bishop was chosen by God.

Still more basic is the intelligent Catholic's questioning of the divine guidance of the hierarchy. I have yet to see the theory of divine guidance openly challenged. Yet almost everywhere its demise is implied. According to this theory, the pope and the bishops are divinely guided. Their decisions are, therefore, said to be according to the "mind of God." While most people are willing to admit their difficulties with the theory of divine appointment, many still feel hesitation in questioning this theory of divine guidance. A realistic view of history shows that the Church like any other institution is guided by a variety of men who range from sincere men of good judgment to genuinely ambitious men of bad judgment. Church history gives clear evidence that the divinely-guided leaders have brought the Church to a position which is almost completely contrary to the spirit of the gospel. A complex system of laws, more detailed and more restrictive than the Mosaic code, governs every aspect of the Catholic's life. An almost incomprehensible liturgy was not only permitted but unflinchingly defended for a thousand years. A clerical caste system was permitted and encouraged. The authoritarian style of dominance is still used to crush any opposition without discussion. The list could be continued, but the point is obvious. If the hierarchy has led the Church to such a posture with divine guidance, we could do as well without it.

Secularized modern man will not blindly accept the proposition that Church leaders are guaranteed divine guidance. Although he may accept the proposition that Christ's Spirit will be in his Church "all days until the end of the world," he finds it impossible to believe that this Spirit is operating only or even best through the judgments of Church leaders. History shows that the hierarchy's statements usually come at the end of a period of development rather than as original new teaching, for example, the Decree on Religious Liberty.

As in every other case where past teachings are submitted to a new critique, someone will arise to object that we have always taught what has now become popular. I recommend that the objector read any manual on obedience dated before 1950 and see if its author does not clearly indicate that one should obey unquestioningly *because* God's will is manifested through one's superior.

The laity's rethinking the theory of authority and obedience and the hierarchy's attempt to rule by the old standards have put the laity and the hierarchy on a collision course. The result has been that the greater the appeal for obedience and the more attempts at control, the less real obedience is achieved. The birth control problem demonstrates these inverse proportional results. The Pope has continued during the past few years to appeal to Catholics to submit to the teaching of "the Church" on birth control. Despite his failure to produce any new, cogent reasons for the Church's condemnation of birth control, he pleads for obedience out of sheer loyalty to his claim upon Catholics as their authoritative guide. Yet fewer and fewer Catholics pay even lip service to the birth control ban. The past two years have seen a similar phenomenon in the matter of liturgy. While Rome continues to condemn unauthorized experiments with the liturgy and laments the ill effects of unapproved experiments, the "bootleg" liturgy continues to blossom everywhere. Again, the more attempt at control, the less real control. The more vaunting of authority, the more the Underground Church grows.

Whereas a generation ago it was still possible for the hierarchy to enforce submission through various forms of control, such is no longer the case. The average adult Catholic has no more concern for the Index of Forbidden Books than he has for the Code of Hammurabi. The whole idea of needing the protection of the hierarchy to prevent his being misled produces not even a protest, but merely a smile. Since the modern Catholic has seen the hierarchy's frequent ineptitude in condemning so many things from short shorts to *Blow-Up,* he feels that it would be foolish to continue to be restricted from those things which are probably the wave of the future. It is an example of how overkill in the use of authority dulls the ability of the subject to hear future commands.

Since Church authority has become too complex and constricting, many Catholics have decided that it is not worth the effort to attempt to secure permissions. When permissions are granted, they are usually loaded down with a whole host of conditions and restrictions. Many feel that the easier and more sensible approach is simply to bypass Church authority and ignore its attempt at control. They decide to live the Christian life and stop wasting time trying to get approval for what can be better done without approval.

Particularly among the young the tendency is not to revolt in violence but simply to ignore the commands of the one in authority since it seems increasingly unimportant to be accepted by the hierarchy. This is well manifested in the Underground Church. Hardly anyone cares to emerge. The disillusionment with the institutional Church has produced an unwillingness to try to deal with it. Perhaps the concern of the Catholic Laymen's Experimental Organization with official recognition is an indication of its conservatism. Perhaps the true wave of the future Church is being manifested in the unstructured, unaccepted, uninhibited Church of the underground.

Finally, it seems that the notion of who is "in" and who is "out" of the Church is being forced into the center of the problem by the attempt to threaten those who fail in obedience with suspension or excommunication. People who come to find a truly meaningful kind of Christian community in an Underground Church begin to question the true meaning of "Church" and to challenge the rights of church authority to declare them out of communion with the Church of Christ because of some legal defect. The strong condemnation of disobedience is especially annoying since the Church at large still neglects to provide strong Christian leadership in areas which are clearly gospel issues.

Liturgy. The immediate attraction of the Underground Church for most people is the new form of liturgy. It is understandable that the informal liturgy of the Underground Church should have a considerable appeal to the concerned Catholic.

The liturgical changes inaugurated in the wake of Vatican II's liturgy Constitution stirred sudden hopes for real involvement in the Mass. Although the revisions came haphazardly, they were for the most part well-received by Catholics. For the first time in their lives they were taking an active part in the Mass. For the first time they could understand directly much of what was being said. A wave of enthusiasm swept over the Church during those first months. Most people were willing to excuse the awkwardness of the new lay leaders and the lack of volume in the singing. There was life and there was hope.

After three years, however, and a few minor rubrical revisions, the mood has changed. The average churchgoer has settled down to reciting the English formulas with as much or as little understanding and enthusiasm as he did the Latin. An English version of the Canon of the Mass has produced no excitement. The English translations of antiquated forms of medieval prayer begin now to grate on the ear and the mind. The monotony of the never-varying routine brings annoyance rather than inspiration. The liturgical changes were merely enough to expose the irrelevance of the Mass formulas in relation to modern life. The alert Catholic is anxious to move on to something more in tune with the rhythms of his real life. Ecclesiastical authority issues only vague hopes of some variants for the future and constantly reiterates its condemnation of any local initiatives as detrimental to "orderly progress." The hopelessness of achieving any significant variation in liturgy through proper channels has created the need for an immediate way of providing variety, spontaneity, and intimacy in the Eucharist. So the people have taken the law into their own hands.

Anyone who reads the gospel account of the Lord's Supper and does a minimum of research on the nature and purpose of signs in the Christian life soon comes to the conclusion that the Sunday liturgy can promote a serious distortion of the meaning of Eucharist in the Christian life. Signs which were intended to represent the closeness of the gracious God have become ritualistic ceremonies completely unrelated to anything common in our experience. If the sign does not signify, it loses its value altogether. A tiny piece of round white matter which neither tastes nor looks like bread can hardly be a sign of nourishment or of a meal of brotherhood. A ritual full of medieval French court gestures is hardly the way to express fellowship between twentieth-century Americans. Nineteenth-century hymnody fails to represent the pace and mood of the technological excitement of our day. Of course, many people would like the Church to be unrelated to daily life. They prefer a religion of solace and otherworldliness. The results of such a liturgy can be seen in the "good Catholics" who threw rocks at Father Groppi as he marched for equal rights for Negroes. Many of those who threw the rocks had never missed Sunday Mass in their lives and probably had received Holy Communion that morning. But if one believes that the Eucharist is the challenge of Christ's love calling his disciples to imitation, the participant expects the eucharistic sign to speak about the Christian concerns of his real life.

The newcomer to an Underground Mass is usually impressed if he is properly prepared. The songs, the language, the gestures, the food and the drink, all are taken from contemporary life. At first one may feel that some of the sacredness is missing. Usually, however, after a few informal Eucharists one begins to sense the real meaning of mystery and of faith. Faith is no longer related to another world but to the mysterious in this world. And here, perhaps, is to be found the greatest long-range effect of the Underground Church.

Faith, which for all too long was described as an intellectual assent to the truths proposed by the Church, is seen as a dynamic encounter with God and with Christ in the midst of life. Faith becomes a way of living rather than a way of thinking. Religion is not about another life but about this one. The demand placed upon the participant in an informal Mass is great. He is called to make an act of faith in the presence of God in the ordinary. The same kind of bread which he uses at his table each day is to be seen as the bearer of Christ to him. A bottle of wine such as he might use for a special family feast becomes the sign of Christ's Blood poured out. The sharing of the Spirit of Christ with other people takes place in the common setting of a home in which people watch television, make love, and argue about their children. The immanence of God becomes a reality.

Inevitably, in such a real-life setting the discussion which forms the heart of the liturgy of the Word turns with great frequency to the social issues of our day. Many have criticized the "new-breed" Christian for excessive emphasis on social issues, and I feel that there is a danger of humanitarianism without transcendence. Yet the gospel message, especially as we hear it in our day, demands a response to the needs of others. If it fails to do so, it fails to relate to the lives of modern men and women. The master whose criterion for judgment day was feeding the hungry, clothing the naked, etc. would certainly be the first to condemn a sacred meal of cozy brotherhood which fails to show concern for those outside the select group.

One of the criticisms of the Underground Church has been that it is self-centered and unconcerned with the needs of the whole Church. It has been my experience, on the contrary, that almost everyone whom I have met from an Underground Church has exhibited a genuine concern for both social needs and the betterment of the Church. If they contribute little in an open way to the growth of the institutional Church, it may be because there is no room provided for the kind of dynamic efforts their community would like to offer. Yet any community with genuine concern for others is contributing something of long-range value to the whole Church, even though it may be concealed for a time.

Although there are some common features to the informal liturgies of the Underground Church, these liturgies are as various as they are widespread. They range from fully-vested services with most of the customary Mass formulas to completely improvised services in which the celebrant dresses like the rest of the community. The basic order of service consists of contemporary music, readings from Scripture and modern literature with discussion, impromptu prayers from the congregation, the Lord's Supper with a prepared or improvised Canon, a kiss of peace, communion with leavened bread and wine, and a concluding prayer and/or hymn. There is that wonderful variety which is essential for the relevance of the liturgical sign to life situations.

With a little thought one can quickly see the absurdity of attempting to formulate a liturgy which will be equally meaningful to natives of the Congo and the suburbanites of Westchester. Nor is the variety necessary only for different cultures. How can one pretend to compose a liturgy which will be of real meaning to an eighty-two-year-old grandmother, a six-

year-old boy, and a young Ph.D. candidate? Just think of the
injustice we have been doing for years to those poor tykes who
have had to sit still for forty-five minutes on benches too high
for their feet to reach the ground and endure a liturgy
which takes some historical background even to recognize, let
alone enter into. There needs to be a special form of Eucharist
for each group as well as variety in the format from occasion
to occasion. To assert that all these varieties would have to be
approved by someone in a Roman Congregation is to indicate
the stranglehold on Church life that Roman overcentralization
has granted itself.

There should be, of course, special liturgies for great occasions when all the people in a spirit of true catholicity gather
to celebrate the oneness they share in Christ. But to make this
single form of celebration the order of the day, or worse, the
only *possible* form, for all people, of all ages, everywhere, is to
ignore the nature of a human sign. Signs proceed from people;
people create them. They are not created by experts and then
performed by a congregation. They are the expression of the
style of life of people where and how they are. The variety and
spontaneity of the Underground Liturgy present the Eucharist
as a "sign of life."

Community. Everyone who joins an Underground Church
is seeking community. As Harvey Cox has so well indicated in
*The Secular City,** modern city-dwellers have a selective
community in which they express their I-Thou relationships.
Toward all others in the vast human community they must
have an I-You relationship. The huge impersonal mass which
constitutes most of our modern Catholic parishes, especially in
the cities, makes any kind of genuine community impossible.
If the Church's role is to help the believer to form a value

* Harvey Cox, *The Secular City* (Macmillan, New York, 1965).

system in accordance with the teachings of Jesus, it must provide a structure in which value formation can effectively occur. The average churchgoer will readily admit that Sunday Mass does not transform his value system. Despite recent liturgical revisions and more vocal participation, the monotony of the Mass formulas and the sense of being lost in the crowd make true *participation* nearly impossible.

The most obvious and immediate asset one experiences in an Underground Church is a true sense of belonging. Unlike the average parish in which neither the priest nor the other parishioners are likely to know one another's name, in an Underground Church all the members soon know one another on a first-name basis and, what is more important, are willing to share their thoughts and souls with one another. Perhaps the members also sense something theologically significant about "naming" each other. The sharing of one person with another on a truly personal basis implies a recognition of the other as a person of value. In the bible great emphasis is given to the name of the person, for knowing the name of a person implies a knowledge of that person's meaning. In the Underground Church people help to define one another's meaning.

A true sense of brotherhood in the Lord is experienced intensely in the eucharistic meal. An experience of the presence of the Spirit of Jesus in the midst of his followers is inevitable in this intimate setting. The binding force which the Spirit provides becomes the source of "community." Theologians have pointed out that the Eucharist *makes* the Christian community. Members of the Underground Church can verify this from experience. The gathering for the Eucharist makes the Church exist. The community *is* the Church.

But all is not sweetness and light. The fact that such communities are forbidden and that serious penalties are visited

upon any priest who dares to celebrate the Eucharist in violation of the rubrics is a source of real anguish to many members of the Underground Church. More importantly, the
condemnation poses serious theological problems. First,
canonically this community is a schismatic church. Do we not,
then, have existing within the Church a secret schismatic
Church unwilling to submit to Rome and the local bishop? For
both Rome and the bishops violently forbid and condemn its
existence. Members of many such Underground Churches, although without much theological training, sense this problem
and live in anguish of spirit because they recognize the delib-
erate disunity which exists. Yet, they are aware that a community which provides them for the first time in their lives
with a valid experience of Christian brotherhood and the possibility of Christian discovery cannot be in opposition to the
mind of Christ. Why, then, should the hierarchy be so violent
in their reiterated condemnation? The laity begin to wonder if
it is the hierarchy who are defecting from the post-Vatican II
Church rather than the opposite.

The second theological problem posed by the existence of
Underground Churches is the meaning of Church membership. For the first time in their lives these Catholics have
"joined" a Church. By canon law they were assigned to the
territorial parish within whose boundaries they lived. Whether
or not their parish church provided a Christian community
life, it was their parish, and they were officially required to
receive all essential sacraments there, be registered, contribute
to its support, etc. The decision to "join a new Church" subtly
demanded that they ask themselves whether they had ever
chosen membership in a Catholic or a Christian Church. The
question which naturally follows is whether or not Christianity
for them is a truly voluntary commitment? All but a small
percentage of Catholics are "born Catholics." Not only did

they not choose Catholicism, but they were actually warned that if they were to "leave" the Church in which they were born, they would "lose their souls." This was clearly evident in the admonitions of a previous generation to send the children to Catholic schools, to avoid mixed marriages and non-Catholic colleges and Protestant services. Protecting one's "faith" meant avoiding the challenge of decision about one's faith. The Underground Church questions some rather basic assumptions of Roman Catholic life. A new understanding of the "community of faith" may ultimately be the most valuable contribution of the Underground Church.

Honesty. One of the striking features of the Underground Church is what we might call instant unanimity. All the members suddenly realize that they share almost all the same basic problems regarding the Church. One member of an Underground Church told me that at the first meeting when the question of confession came up for discussion, each one in the group admitted that he had not been to confession for over a year. Yet, all continue to receive Communion without any hesitation. Members experience a great feeling of relief to know that they are not alone in their doubts and difficulties about Catholic teachings and practices. The remarkable thing is that there is such universal agreement instantly. The obvious inadequacy of many Catholic practices which had produced an individualized, interior revolt is finding articulation in the Underground Churches. The ferment which makes the Underground Church both possible and necessary has been churning in the souls of serious Catholics for years. The irrelevancies of Catholic doctrine and practice which were patiently borne in secret have become suddenly open for discussion in a group of kindred spirits.

It is interesting to recall that a similar kind of instant

unanimity was experienced by the bishops at Vatican II. Men who had secretly held liberal views of theology suddenly became aware that they were not alone. The open declarations of some of the more courageous bishops and cardinals at the opening session gave others the strength to unite against the formerly unassailable position of the Curia. Although most of the documents of Vatican II emerged as rather conservative, compromise statements of twentieth-century theological development, the experience of being able to stand up against the powerful Roman control and speak one's mind was a liberating experience for the Church at large.

Perhaps, however, what the Catholic member of the Underground enjoys most is the opportunity for honesty and integrity in the openness of the Underground Church. Perhaps for the first time in his life he is able to express what *he* believes. The teaching authority of the Church was so constantly stressed as the source of one's beliefs that the Catholic felt compelled to repress any disagreement for fear of being considered heretical. In the Underground one can express his beliefs or rejection of accepted belief without fear of shocking others. He can expect that his opinions will be given a respectful hearing and corrected or corroborated by the viewpoints of other members of the group. What a marvelous feeling of relief it is to be able to expose those nagging doubts to the light and to find that others share similar problems and are willing to share in the search for honest solutions!

Priests who belong to Underground groups are listened to with respect and their opinions valued, but the position of the priest as the one who gives the "answer" after the children have tried their best is no longer the case. Often *his* doubts find some resolution from the insights of the lay members of the group. The distinction between the teaching Church and the listening Church completely dissolves in the honest exchange that takes place in the Underground Church.

As was suggested above, the intelligent Catholic no longer feels subject to the intellectual controls provided by censorship. If he has read Harvey Cox, John A. T. Robinson, Gabriel Vahanian, or Joseph Fletcher, or even serious reviews of these books, he has fallen under the spell of the "secular" theologians. It is no longer possible for him to think in terms of the pious Catholicism of his parents. He no longer cares about indulgences, votive candles, novenas, scapulars, Fatima, and a host of other devotions which formed the basis of Catholic piety twenty years ago. Not only that, but he actually rejects some doctrines which were considered beyond question a few years ago, for example, the necessity of auricular confession, papal authority as an absolute guide to conscience, the physical virginity of Mary, the description of the Catholic Church as the one, true Church. The Catholic who has such doubts desperately needs a community in which he can feel free to search for truth in honesty and where he can be accepted as a searcher, rather than being required to take an either/or position regarding doctrinal statements about which he is uncertain. He wants freedom to search for what is relevant in the ancient truths and freedom to jettison what is obsolete.

The Future. The Underground Church is for me a sign of great hope and great fear. The very fact that people care enough to seek for some more valid form of community in which to search for greater commitment is very heartening. That they should do so in violation of the restrictions of their religious leaders seems even more admirable, for it indicates a maturity of personal conviction which far outvalues the "crime" of disobedience. That priests should be willing to risk their personal and professional security in order to provide for the real needs of their people seems also heartening. It well may be that from this disorder and disobedience may emerge a new understanding between the hierarchy, the clergy, and the laity which will furnish a model for a truly unified people of God. Such sincere zeal can hardly fail to produce lasting fruit for the Community of Christ.

The catacomb Church of the Sixties, however, is also a cause of real anxiety. That so much sincere good will and zeal should have to remain underground speaks ill for the leadership in the Church. Unless Church leaders soon begin to make use of the potential being siphoned off into the Underground and unless the local hierarchy soon find the courage to speak clearly to Roman authorities about the needs of their people, the very best and most committed people are going to be lost to the institutional Church. The condition of alienation which exists is considered temporary by almost everyone in the Underground Church. If, however, signs of bold new steps by the hierarchy are not soon forthcoming, I fear that many are going to be lost to the Church through disgust and disillusionment. The Underground Church, unlike the Church of the first century, cannot bear to remain underground for long. In the first century the persecution came from the pagans and gave a spirit of unity to those who were banded together against the persecutors of God's people. When, in the present situation, the persecution proceeds from those who are supposed to be the leaders of God's people, the disaffection will soon make hierarchy-laity communication impossible, and the acephalous Underground Church will begin to disintegrate with the consequent loss of many zealous people.

The attempt by the Catholic Laymen's Experimental Organization to bring the matter to a head and call for a general emergence of the Underground with the consequent resolution of the problem seems at this writing to have failed. Perhaps it is because the timing was wrong. Too many are still too timid. Or perhaps the Underground is not meant to emerge. At any rate I believe the Underground Church is a passing stage in Church history, witnessing to a tragic communications gap between the Church *politique* and the Church *mystique*.

11 / Emmaus: A Venture
in Community
and Communication

by DAVID KIRK

The crisis facing today's Church goes beyond the issue of definition. Even if we could reach a consensus on definition, even if we agreed that the Church should be a servant people whose ministry was to the world, the question of the adequacy of present forms and structures would remain. Is the residential parish a suitable basis from which to tackle the massive issues of the emerging city and to make community? If the layman ought to be the first in the Church's prophetic ministry, what structures and forms will he choose to keep or reshape? Is the Church as presently structured equipped to enter the world of reality? Is Catholicism too institutionalized to permit meaningful change? Should we work for renewal within the institution or should we conclude, as many have, that the present forms of Catholicism have no future at all? How can an eighteenth-century Christian participate in a twenty-first-century human revolution?

Emmaus House is an experiment exploring these issues and seeking to break through to the new land. It amounts to a test of ourselves, a test of the Church, a call to faith. It means risking ourselves to the unknown and putting all truths to the test. It amounts to becoming a fellow searcher with the rest of man, "as one beggar who tells the other beggar where to find bread."

We know that not only our society has gone afloat, but Chistians have as well. In our consciousness we have become mobile and in exodus. We are continually on the way in our thinking, always questioning, without necessarily seeking a point of rest or a terminal point of our thinking in a final answer.

This process of faith implies a rejection of those forms of religion which are an occasion of idolatry, which become a cave where one escapes from the presence of the living and free God. For our God is not a temple dweller. He advances through time. Again and again he lets the new conquer the old. He is not the God of the status quo, but rather is the Lord of the future, history, and the world. Living a life of faith for Emmaus means exposing ourselves to the endless new doings of God in the secular world. In Bonhoeffer's phrase, it means enduring reality before God.

In 1960, David Kirk and Lyle Young met in Rome during theological studies at the Beda College. David had his roots in a Catholic Worker background and Lyle came from ten years' work as a freewheeling Episcopal priest in New Guinea. They came to the conclusion that, generally speaking, parish ministry was *irrelevant,* because it did not speak adequately to life situations and spoke only weakly to "private life" rather than to public issues; *ineffective,* since a post-ecclesiastical world no longer has a need of a "traveling salesman in solemnities"; *morally ambiguous,* for social pressures push the priest toward caution, compromise, and, worst of all, self-deception. The whole social structure of the parish and the priesthood seemed a very dead remnant of the eighteenth century. It belonged to a rural, preindustrial community where it was practical and useful.

David and Lyle wanted to seek out new forms of communication and ministry, across the boundaries of dogmatic traditions, which would approach men at the point of their secular strength and crisis situations.

The experimental idea was presented to Patriarch Maximos, head of the worldwide Melkite Catholic community—considered at the time to be the "left wing" of the Catholic Church—and later to the American Melkite Exarch, Bishop Justin.[1] Eventually, in September, 1966, David, Lyle, and a group of companions bought an old brownstone on 116th Street, New York City, near their friends at the East Harlem Protestant Parish.

Although the priests have permission of their Melkite bishop to found and staff the center, the Melkite Exarchate has a "hands off" policy in regard to the happenings at Emmaus. "It is an experiment," Father John Jadaa, the Melkite chancellor, has said to the press, "and we are studying it and watching it carefully." The Archdiocese of New York has only indicated publicly that it has "reservations about the experimental nature of Emmaus."

Dr. Hokendijk, of Union Theological Seminary and one of our advisers, has suggested that the Churches have always lived with bookkeeping that had a double entry: strict and closed in normal situations, free and open in abnormal situations. We are convinced that there are no "normal times" for the Christian or the Church and, therefore, nonessential rules

[1] The Melkite Bishops at the Vatican Council, and after, consistently presented the more open (thus biblical) approaches to Church structure, liturgy, priesthood, birth control, clerical celibacy, modern warfare, etc.

are obsolete. "Normal times" persuade the Church that moral crisis is not her ideal climate, that her task is to sanctify the status quo.

And what is Emmaus?

We are a *community of Christians* who are seeking to join totally in the lives and struggles of the human community.

We are an *ecumenical center of renewal* seeking new and relevant structures around human needs and human issues.

COMMUNITY

As a community we are concerned with renewal of the world and the Church and seek to work toward this renewal.

The community is both residential and nonresidential. The residential group makes a commitment for a year and lives in Emmaus House or nearby in apartments. The members of the community range in age from twenty-two to forty-five; they include a social worker and a teacher who work in East Harlem, the director of a Catholic international student movement, a Blessed Sacrament Father, a writer, and the two founders. They meet each evening for a community meal and on Thursday evening for a community meeting. Each member contributes what he can to the support of the community. The nonresidential group comes together each Sunday for the Eucharist, discussion, and friendship.

The Emmaus community is fluid in terms of membership since this kind of group changes. Leadership is reduced to its simplest expression. David Kirk is Coordinator, bringing together the various elements in communal growth. Before final decisions are made at Emmaus, they are discussed by the group as a whole. Informality, flexibility, and spontaneity are characteristic.

We need *brothers* who continually carry to us words of friendship and who are joined through our common commitment to Christ and to others.

Together, we seek to *be* the Church of Jesus Christ, which is "where two or three are gathered together in his name." We feel that the Church can no longer witness corporately as a community. So we must think more in terms of the Church in small *koinonia* groups. Faced with a Church which so often is building-centered—our money, time, and life are sometimes centered around Church buildings and organizations, and the "good layman" is one who is linked with this kind of institutionalism—we are saying that a return to the cellular structure of the Church is a necessity for its life. As exemplified by the early Church, which was lived and spread by house-communities, any community which comes together with the basic elements for "Church" (Acts 2:42)—fellowship, teaching, prayer, the Breaking of the Bread—*is* the Church in its fullness.

But we also feel that in order to be an effective Christian communal witness, Christians must meet today in ad-hoc situations, outside denominations, around actual human needs.

SEEKING A NEW STYLE OF CHRISTIAN LIVING

At Emmaus, we are seeking a style of living which comes from our understanding of what the Church, holiness, and the world are about. This means a radical reworking of some of our past assumptions.

There are few guidelines for us. There are no final answers. But there seems to be a consensus among us which provides clues to a style of life. These signposts seem to call us to be:

Secular, postreligious. The present world provides creative ground for man's moral and cultural values. The call to secularity is a refusal to be dominated by religious practices which try to make God do our bidding (Matt. 23:1-2) and a refusal to live as slaves to custom and superstition when we have been freed to be sons of God (Gal. 4:1-7).

Joining mankind in its life. Freed from religious myth, the Christian may find genuine solidarity with non-Christians, such as the Hindu, the agnostic or the Communist, in striving together toward the common task of building up a genuinely human society.

The gospel calls us to join with all men in the process of humanization, that is, the Christian must make common cause with all those movements and individuals which wish to promote "liberation from the fetters of sacred tradition, together with the renewal of society in the direction of a truly secular and man-made order of life." Whatever the immediate crises of our community and world, be they poverty, peace, or a new school bus, we must take responsibility to see men's needs and then, with other concerned men, to act in an appropriate and expedient manner to bring about justice and freedom for those involved. Further, it is clear that living together implies a mutual communication and dialog. We discover ourselves in this process of helping, with other men, to define and create a whole community.

Searching for an authentic human life. This life will be existence-centered, meaning-centered. Not that this is new: in the early Church, the prayer "Lord, have mercy" did not mean "Forgive me my sins," but "Help me in my existence." The symbol of this life will be Jesus the man. The structure? We don't know, and we do not think that it matters much so long as it is real and authentic for the persons involved. Dr. Hokendijk says: "We must remember the past in terms of liberating joy; we must live the present in terms of trust; we must accept the future in terms of confidence and hope, refusing the utopia of the status quo."

Seeking freedom with a limit. We feel that we are free for the future. But we are free for others; this is the only limit to freedom. And we are free for the gospel, which supplies the freedom for choice and decision and provides the outlook which drives the world on as history.

People whose prayer is a part of existence and life. Monasticism has structured our prayer life to the point of a complete lack of spontaneity. We are seeking a kind of unstructured common prayer—"praying always in the Spirit"—where there is complete freedom to have silence or a reading or a vocal prayer, as the individuals involved might be moved.

The same with the Eucharist, which is especially the sacrament of Christian prayer. We are seeking a sense of celebration of the Eucharist as simple as possible, using the one cup and the one loaf as a symbol of the fact that we are glad to be one and to love one another.

In the liturgy, we give everyone a chance to talk and make announcements about the activities of the week, to ask for prayers, and to tell about items of mutual interest, such as a housing rally, a meeting, or a birthday. By the time we finish sharing our lives together, the Eucharist seems more like our offering, our concern. We give one another a handshake or embrace of peace. Everyone goes around and shakes everyone else's hand to make them welcome.

Worship, then, becomes a way of breaking down barriers.

Another way of celebrating is to act out the parts of the service, so that they can be seen and felt. For example, in the East Harlem Protestant Parish the meal that acts out the event of the Last Supper on Holy Thursday is worth a hundred articles about the doctrine of the Eucharist. A folk-rock pas-

sion play on Good Friday is a reverent way of teaching the life
of Christ. Instead of "foot washing" on Holy Thursday, we
kneel down and polish the shoes of the people.

The celebration of *confession* has several times been an
opportunity for us to gather together and make confession of
sin and faith to one another. Anyone who has ever been part
of a community knows how difficult this is. Yet it becomes a
way of becoming really yourself before your brother.

Bible study together is a part of the joint projects of the
East Harlem Protestant Parish and Emmaus House. We have
found in the Parish that the weekly bible study group is so
important for mutual growth in understanding of the bible, of
self, and of the problems of community. The Parish puts out
its own lectionary for study and teaching.[2]

COMMUNITY SERVICE TO OTHERS

Fellowship and community can become idols without evolving
into service to others. And we have tried to think in terms of
response to needs of others rather than of blueprints and vast
plans to "save" others. Bonhoeffer wrote, "The Church is her
true self only when she exists for others." We think the time
has come for us to renounce any claim to clerical domination
or any attempt to "churchify" the world. We have realized
that the true attitude of Christians to the world is one of service.

The community began in East Harlem with just the idea of
being present day-in and day-out, without labels, in an available manner.

Gradually, the house has become a *house of hospitality* for
those who were lonely, who had no place to sleep or eat, who

---

[2] Commentary by the Rev. Letty Russel of the East Harlem Protestant
Parish.

could not find a job. Our guests have included a young Negro boy who had been thrown out of his home down the block, a SNCC worker just arrived in New York City, a conscientious objector trying to find work, and some young men who had heard about the house in Ecuador and arrived with baggage and not a word of English at three o'clock in the morning. There is always a small but consistent number of temporary guests.

East Harlem students came to the house and asked if we knew anyone who could tutor them. Kathy Mahon, one of our members, had directed a tutorial program in West Harlem and responded to this situation by starting the *Emmaus Tutorial Remedial Reading Program* on Saturdays and after school.

Others have come to the house with both psychological problems and the mere difficulty of coping with urban life (police, welfare, legal difficulties, etc.). In response, Lyle Young and Muriel Zimmerman have started the *Emmaus Counseling Service* (connected with the Interfaith Counseling Service and Metropolitan Hospital), and Charles Emmett, an attorney, has made himself available for free legal service.

Other members of the group work within present structures in the East Harlem community and elsewhere: teaching in a school, working as a community organizer in the poverty program, etc.

Members of the Emmaus community are encouraged, in the tradition of the East Harlem Protestant Parish, to recognize politics and social action as part of their Christian responsibility. The disciplines of the Parish require that each member take an active part in one or more community activities or organizations working for the improvement of East Harlem and all of New York City. For example, one member is on the People's Board of Education, a unit attempting to bring about more community participation in the schools. Lyle Young works closely with established mental health centers, fostering better facilities in East Harlem.

The manner is that of a *task force,* with our energies focused upon problems and people, rather than upon the maintaining of buildings and permanent projects. The point is that perhaps more important than some antipoverty programs are small groups of Christians and others who seek to be available day after day. Real transformation comes through "little people doing little things."

EMMAUS: CENTER FOR ECUMENICAL PARTICIPATION IN THE LIFE OF THE WORLD

Besides the fact that Emmaus is a new kind of community, beyond traditional boundaries, it is also a center working to break down barriers which exist in the world and in the Church. Emmaus House in New York City is used for smaller living-room conferences and hospitality, and Emmaus-on-the-Road in Putnam Valley, New York, provides space for larger conferences and meetings, bringing people together to discuss topics of concern.

We are frank and direct about our position: denominationalism is obsolete. "Institutional ecumenism" is not our interest. Rather we are more interested in a personal, secular ecumenism which leads us through the world to joint action— a kind of loyal opposition to "churchly ecumenism." The new forms and new structures we seek to develop begin with the assumption that the Church is one in Jesus Christ and that men and women should go past structures to build a more truly human community in search of a style of life.

There are many ecumenical centers in the United States, but, as far as we know, the only similar group to Emmaus is the Shalom group in the Netherlands. Both Shalom and Emmaus have common world-centered perspectives. Both would probably characterize many of the ecumenical experiments of the past as too churchy, too clerical. Both attempt to be the "Church inside out"—emphasizing "being the Church in the world" rather than the institution, emphasizing the servant-nature of the Church rather than cult and ritual, working faithfully in the world in the hopeful anticipation of the fulfillment of peace on earth.

During our first year at Emmaus House we had thirty-eight conferences bringing together small groups with diverse barriers: Christians of different confessions, Christians and Marxists, clergy and laymen, urban and suburban men, hawks and doves. The purpose of the meetings for such diverse groups of people has been to lead us to a new and deeper understanding of ourselves, our brothers, and the common problems and opportunities we face. In some cases, these dialog situations have resulted in new forms of life and action: an experimental parish, a committee for rethinking the meaning of the priesthood, a parents-teachers education meeting, and so on. Thus, the role of Emmaus is to be a catalyst.

Like the Shalom community, a small group of Catholics and Protestants and others meet together in agape meals. The leading of the agape meal is shared by the whole group. The order is flexible, and the theme will be relevant to the concerns of the community. During the meal bread is broken and wine is poured, and these are given to each one present. Dialog takes place on the road to Emmaus, and the bread gives strength along the way.

Emmaus is also a cooperating ministry of the East Harlem Protestant Parish, an ecumenical parish with freedom to seek "new wineskins" for the life of the world. We have a joint staff meeting and come together in common prayer, bible study, and worship, and do task force work in community action.

FOR RADICAL SOCIAL CHANGE

Because issues continue to thrust themselves at us in these times of revolution, we find that our calling is to go the way of social revolution.

We feel that the search for orienting theories and the creation of human values is complex but worthwhile. Looking at the past, we have no sure formulas, no tested theories. But we are guided by the radical implications of the gospel. We find its modern application particularly in the *New Left,* which would replace power rooted in possession, privilege, and circumstances with power and uniqueness rooted in love, reflectiveness, and creativity.

With others on the radical left, we are very much concerned in the building up of a revolutionary consciousness in the Church and in the world. With the Catholic Worker, we are convinced that the process of radicalization leads to an understanding that voting, for example, has nothing to do with changing one's life. It is choosing between alternatives provided by someone else. A radical conception of society sees the necessity for people to undergo a reevaluation of their society. Malcolm X would say, it's "telling it like it is." This leads to a disengagement from existing institutions, rejecting the rewards and demands of that society in order to clear the ground for a new conception of society. Rejection of those established values creates the need for new values and new sources of human relationships built in community and understanding rather than in alienation, estrangement, and distrust.

Once a person has made a break with traditional politics, it is important that he find his way with other men to mount the challenge to tottering liberal reform. He must find out how black people live and what the political realities of the ghetto are; he must find out how the poor survive and what a solution to their problems would entail; he must find out how schools are run in the cities, how police treat people who don't have connections, what happens to people on welfare, why kids tune in, turn on, and drop out. That experience, far removed from the sanctuary or slick campaign slogans, provides a beginning for a radical solution to American problems.

We at Emmaus have had to overcome our own concern for "respectability" before we could see how unrespectable the fabric of American life is. What does it mean for the Church to show its "solid citizens" in Harlem? What about the junkies, prostitutes, pushers, pimps, winos, queers, and hustlers? How will we deal with the obscenities we have created?

There is a vision emerging for renewal and human revolution among young people. Emmaus is able to have something to do, at least in a small way, with that radical rethinking only because it grooves, if you will, on that new vision.

How does it all happen? The members of the residential community do all the cooking, cleaning, writing, printing, correspondence, talking with visitors; some of these members work at the house after leaving a regular day-job. No one is paid a salary at Emmaus House; everything is voluntary. Everyone pitches in and Emmaus "happens."

We try to share with others what we are experiencing, even though our experiment may not be adaptable in every comparable situation. The services include a magazine, *The Bread is Rising* (the word of hope whispered among the poor at the time of the French Revolution), bulletins, conferences, hospitality and information to visitors, weekly meetings with resource people and visitors from other parts of the nation and the world, consultation and advice for local ecumenical groups and task forces, and a speakers' service when called upon.

We are trying to walk in the freedom of Abraham's faith, out of the oppression of our closed and too clubby little world and into open air and open history, into the middle of ultimate realities. Where are we going? We don't know. But we do know that our God is not a temple dweller, not a god of the status quo, but the Lord of the future, of the world, of history. We can hope because there is the future where man grows, evolves, becomes.

12/ Litany
from the Underground, II

by ROBERT W. CASTLE, JR.

Leader: O God, the peace that passes understanding,
Response: Help us to understand.
             O God, all men living together in love and peace,
                Help us to love peace.
             O God, who is hung up in this terrible war in Vietnam,
                Help us to get out.
             O God, who is a civilian blown to bits by the bombs which someone said were only meant to destroy military targets,
                Help us to stop the war.
             O God, who wanders alone, lost, crying, scared, no speech from mouth after your mother and father were ripped to death before your eyes,
                Help us to stop the war.
             O God, who is sold for a lousy buck as a sweet whore in Saigon, and dies every night and hates her murderers,
                Help us to stop the war.
             O God, who staggers from village to village, hut to hut, cave to cave, unable to outrace destruction,

Help us to stop the war.

O God, whose town, his village, his family, his friends, his children, his land, his crops, his home, are no more,

Help us to stop the war.

O God, who has a phony election determined by the sword and not the vote,

Help us to stop the war.

O God, who is a flunkie, taking in some wash, polishing some boots, stealing some supplies, to survive, and is dead inside,

Help us to stop the war.

O God, who has troops and tanks and planes in your land to protect you from yourself,

Help us to stop the war.

O God, who has the self-appointed policeman of the world ravaging you and your land,

Help us to change the Nation.

O God, who is used as the reason for escalating a Third World War, the whim of the militants and fascists of our day,

Help us to change the Nation.

O God, who is enticed with a chocolate bar in the hand and a knife in the back,

Help us to stop the war.

O God, who has seen his cities become vile, filthy, corrupt, run for the advantage of your supposed liberators,

Help us to stop the war.

O God, who is blasphemed by this holocaust of killing,

Help us to stop the killing.

O God, who is a number every day in the local paper or on the TV screen, 19 of us, 127 of them,

Help us stop the killing.

O God, who is us and them?

Help us to be.

O God, who is poor and couldn't find a job in the Great Society and got shipped to Vietnam to kill the poor,

Help us to change our sick society.

O God, who is black, put on the front line to kill people of color because we don't discriminate when it comes to killing,

Help us to change our sick society.

O God, who is called "nigger" in the land of the free and the brave, and a freedom fighter in Vietnam,

Help us to change our sick society.

O God, whose black body is twisted still in death in some rice paddy, for free elections in Vietnam, and swinging softly from some tree in the United States because he went to vote in a free election,

Help us to change our sick society.

O God, who is sold a phony bill of goods that he is fighting for democracy and freedom,

Help us to change our sick society.

O God, whose country fights war in the name of self-determination and allows none to the poor of its own land,

Help us to change our sick society.

O God, who has been duped into the paranoia of killing human beings who are called communist instead,

> Help us to change our sick society.

O God, who has sold out peace and love and humanity in the name of pride, nationalism, flag waving, support the boys, boys, drop the bomb, kill the Gooks,

> Help us to change.

O God, who is hung up knowing the war is wrong but we're there and can't see any way out and the war grows and grows,

> Help us to change.

O God, who hates the war, its sickness, its immorality, the unjustness, the calamity, and folly, and is afraid to speak out and act out peace,

> Help us to change you.

O God, who died on the hill, came home in the box, and is now ashes to ashes for what?

> Help us to see you.

O God, who receives a telegram, a visit in uniform, and the words, we are sorry, your son,

> Help us to know you.

O God, fighting to survive, kill or be killed, and know it's all sick and wrong,

> Help us to know you.

O God, who is told day after day that we seek peace and negotiation, and rain bombs on Haiphong and Hanoi,

> Help us to cut out the phony stuff.

O God, who believes we want negotiations and self-determination, when in reality we want surrender and our own way,

    Help us not to be phony.

O God, whose country has made a mockery, and destroyed the United Nations of the world,

    Help us to change the Nation.

O God, whose government has the whole world in fear and terror of impending disaster.

    Help us to change the Nation.

O God, whose government labels those who seek peace, who dissent from their policy as simplistic traitor, giving aid and comfort to the enemy,

    Help us to change the people.

O God, who hears the thunder of war in Vietnam and the silence for freedom in South Africa and Rhodesia,

    Help us to seek freedom.

O God, whose churches too often close their eyes, bless the war, pray for victory in Jesus' name,

    Help us to change the Church.

O God, who is told the war is holy, righteous, some kind of divine mission to set the people free,

    Help us out of the con game.

O God, who seeks peace and refuses to be called into the army to learn how to search and destroy and raise the kill ratio,

    Help us to love peace.

O God, who is joining together with others to find ways to end the war and love peace,

    Help us to organize.

O God, who has marched the streets to bring the troops home, to stop the bombing, to negotiate, to give Vietnam back to the Vietnamese, to stop the killing, to stop the war,

Help us to love peace.

O God, who is organizing to bring some sanity, some love, some understanding among the people of the nations and the world,

Help us to love peace.

O God, who would run the risks of peace and not the risks of war,

Help us to stop the war.

O God, who loves his country and is horrified to see what it is, and protests in the hope of changing the nation and its people,

Help us to stop the war.

O God, who has seen the urgency of the day and will risk all, for peace,

Help us to stop the war.

O God, who burns his draft card and loves freedom,

Help us to love freedom.

O God, who is a pacifist and conscientious objector, and loves peace,

Help us to love peace.

O God, who burns the flag and loves people,

Help us to love people.

O God, who refuses to kill his brother in war and sits and rots in prison,

Help us to stay strong.

O God, who talks to his neighbor, people at work

and on the street, to encourage love and peace
between nations of the world,
>Help us to spread the word.

O God, all men, women and children who in their
own beautiful way work for peace,
>Help us to stop the war.

O God, all men, women and children who would
like to work for peace and are afraid,
>Help us to join the peacemakers.

O God, the peacemaker,
>Blessed are the peacemakers.

Minister: O God, I see you,
People: O God, you're crying,
Minister: O God, you're wounded,
People: O God, you're bleeding,
Minister: O God, you're dying,
People: O God, you're dead.
Minister: Long live God!
People: Long live God!

13/ The Missionary and the Black Man

by SPEED B. LEAS

We do-gooders have been put in one of the most difficult positions our ilk has ever been in. We have lost the vision—if you will, the ideology—that at one time made it possible for us to unabashedly be about our reforming (or, is that word "redeeming") task in the world. Just a short time ago we were confident that our task was the integration of the black man into a system that whirled on by him, often unconcerned about but just as often hostile to his advancement. We were confident that blacks were disadvantaged, deprived, and/or excluded, and that our task was well-defined in two words: "integration" and "training."

Blacks, however, have not been appreciative of our efforts to improve their lot. They have made it seem that we have been about the wrong task in the wrong way. Stokely Carmichael in a speech to the students at the University of California in Berkeley on November 19, 1966 compared our good efforts with those of the missionaries in Africa.[1] He said, ". . . they come into our ghettos and they . . . Head Start, upward lift, bootstrap, and upward bound us into white society." The American colonists "have been feeding us the thalidomide drug

[1] Reprinted in the Key List Mailing, San Francisco Regional Office of the Student Nonviolent Coordinating Committee, December 11, 1966.

of integration, and . . . some Negroes have been down a dream
street talking about sitting next to white people, and that does
not begin to solve the problem. We were never fighting for the
right to integrate, we were fighting against white supremacy."
He continued:

For example, the missionaries were sent to Africa; they went with
the attitude that blacks were automatically inferior. As a matter
of fact the first act the missionaries did, you know, when they got
to Africa was to make us cover up our bodies because they said it
got them excited. We couldn't go bare breasted anymore because
they got excited. Now when the missionaries came to civilize us
because we were uncivilized, educate us because we were uneducated, and give us some literature studies because we were illiter-
ate, they charged a price. The missionaries came with the Bible,
and we had the land. When they left, they had the land, and we
still have the Bible.

To sensitive people Carmichael's message is clear in its
damning of our failure to avoid colonialism, and we do not
know what to do. We have seen how our welfare system tends
to foster and encourage dependency; we have seen how the
integration movement has not really dealt with the problem of
white superiority when it puts the black man in a position of
begging for what is rightfully his and the white man in the
position of gratuitously handing out tokens of integration; we
have seen how our efforts for job equality have barely touched
the surface of unequal employment; we have seen how our
laws against discrimination in the schools have done little to
change their segregated pattern North and South. Nobody,
yet, has really come up with a satisfying solution to how we
are going to deal with our failures without falling into the
same traps that have already kept us from getting amywhere

with our good intentions. We stand in confusion before our failures. And the blacks in the New Movement (Black Power/ Nationalism) are telling us that we are no longer either wanted or needed. Whitey has made such a mess of things that he should get out and let the black man get himself together.

The New Movement is saying some things that we missionaries need to hear, and hear very clearly. In the first place, as we mentioned above, it is saying that whites should get out of the black ghettos. A substantial part of the black man's problem is that he has accepted the white racist's view of blackness, the nationalists are telling us. The black man has accepted the white conception of blackness as symbolic of inferiority. Kinky hair, large noses, thick lips, dark skin: all of these things are seen by Negro children as something to be ashamed of. The leadership of the black community that is not black tends to enhance the Negro child's picture of goodness as identified with other than black images. The child identifies leadership with whiteness and dependency with blackness. The nationalist says that for the child to appreciate himself and his race, he needs to have black leaders, black teachers, and black professionals with whom he can identify. He tells us that one of the major problems of the person in the black ghetto is the guilt and shame he feels just because he is black. The black child does not see black people with whom he would like to identify and consequently comes to believe in his own inferiority. He denies his heritage, he denies his own potential, he denies any sense of his own worth, and therefore he does not try to become anything other than his own negative image of himself. Believing only whites can make it, he does not try to make it for himself.

More than pointing out the need for black leadership in his own community, however, the black nationalist tells us, in the second place, that the growing child should see black *male* leadership. A large part of the black man's lack of initiative and will to better himself comes from the submission that he feels not only because of his blackness but also because of the matriarchal structure of the family in the ghetto. For a man to feel himself a man without neurotic responses overcompensating for his uncertainty that being male is a good thing, children should see effective black men at work exerting male leadership in the community and in the home. Not only does the matriarchal nature of the poor black family hamper the male's ability to appreciate himself, but it is especially debilitating when all the images of a successful family which he sees in the rest of the society are based on a weakening, but still fairly strong, patriarchal system. Consequently, he is always slightly off balance and confused as to what his role is and how he will fulfill it.

In the third place, the New Movement is telling us that what was intended to be a helpful system for alleviating the plight of the poor has only increased their powerlessness. What has happened is that those of us who have been concerned about the plight of the deprived in our community, in our zeal to meet their immediate physical needs, have lost sight of the democratic right of every person to pursue his own destiny. Instead of meeting the immediate physical needs and providing the support, technical assistance, and ability to participate fully in the rest of the society, we have merely put bandages on the sore (that is, symptoms) and done nothing to alleviate its causes. Our welfare programs, school systems, Church missions, and political endeavors have all been aimed at doing *for* rather than helping to make it possible for the poor to do for themselves. And this kind of welfarism leads to greater and greater dependency.

Another thing that the New Movement is telling us is that

the best way to fight this increasing dependency is no longer to look to integration as the goal of the black self-improvement movement. The immediate task must be the improvement of the black community. Only after the blacks have gotten themselves together, can they begin to negotiate (and then on equal terms) for equity in the Great Society.

Finally, the New Movement is telling us that the more inclusive goal of saving the white man from his own white supremacist ethic, which was clearly the goal of the Civil Rights movement that nonviolently tried to shame the white man into more equitable behavior, cannot be primary. The New Movement's posture is now one of self-defense; its motto might be "Don't tread on me"; and its recommendation to the white community is "Tend to your own business; we'll tend to ours." In the past the Civil Rights movement sought to save the white man from the sin of racism as it freed the black man. The New Movement assumes that if each movement tends to its own proper business, equity will come.

While much of what we see coming out of the Black Power movement must be affirmed, the Christian missionary is hard put to condone ethically or tactically a good deal of what we are seeing. There is no questioning the powerlessness of the majority of the blacks in this nation and their legitimate need for power, nor do we deny the debilitating paternalism that has characterized this nation's and its Churches' policy at home and abroad. We are also brought up clearly to the problem of the Negro's self-depreciating victim-image of himself and his people. Nonetheless, we are struck by the failure of the Black Power stance to adequately deal with the real world of which it is a part.

In a very real sense the Black Power/Nationalism stance of

the New Movement is a Neo-Puritanism. Here we are not referring to the stringent moralism vis-à-vis sexuality (though a good deal of this is found particularly among the Muslims), but rather to the pervasive "You-can-make-it-if-you-work-hard-enough-individualism" that is characteristic of the whole Movement. There is almost a blatant denial on the part of the leadership of the Black Power movement, in almost every quarter, of the complexity of intra- and inter-group dependency within this society and the social, psychological, economic, and other forces that push and pull at individuals and groups. Much like the New England Puritan at the beginning of our country, black nationalists seem to have an unwavering belief that since their cause is right, somehow everything will work itself out. Individual initiative and self-help become the main focus of the Movement with little calculation of the effects of the movements of the larger society or the effect of such an ethic on those whose circumstances simply will not allow the individualistic, self-help doctrine to be a real, viable alternative.

Out of this Neo-Puritanism is developing an image of manliness that is not unlike that of the Western movie. Few would deny that the predominant American image of what it means to be a man has been stongly influenced by the unemotional, hard-hitting cowboy who can and will use any means to strike down and utterly destroy evil which is always embodied in another human being. The good guy is all good and the bad guy is all bad, and it is no loss to anyone when the bad guy is killed in a shoot-out or hung from a hastily erected gallows on the main street of town.

But this American image of what it means to be a man is on the wane, we are told by observers of American culture. Mc-Luhan and Leonard in the July 25, 1967 issue of *Look* magazine have this to say:

It takes a particularly obstinate blindness not to realize that an ability to free emotions, and not a fragmented "all-maleness," provides today's most compelling erotic appeal.

We might also confess that our reading of the new teen-age "conformity" of dress and hairdo fails to consider the social ritualism of these forms. They express the new desire for depth involvement in social life rather than egotistic eccentricity.

The trend (perhaps without the exaggerated hair style) seems likely to continue. The all-sensory, all-pervasive total environment of the future may be no place for the narrow-gauge, specialized male. Emotional range and psychic mobility may be valued. Heightened intuition may be required. The breed of hombre generally portrayed by John Wayne is already an anachronism. "Be a man!" the hombre bellows, and the more perceptive of our young laugh.

And if the narrow-gauge male is not laughed out of existence, he may, literally, *die* out.[2]

This raises the most perplexing question of all for the Black Power movement: Is the movement preparing the black outcast for a life style which is dead or dying or is it preparing the black man to live in the emerging postmodern era? Is all the to-do about the negative effects of matriarchal culture in a predominantly patriarchal system an anachronism? Is the Black Power movement asking for the black man to become something that, if and when he achieves it, will no longer be a viable life style?

We must ask another question of the goals of the New Movement. LeRoi Jones tells us that Nationalism is the only way the black man can go. In an essay in his book *Home* on "The Legacy of Malcolm X" he tells us:

[2] Marshall McLuhan and George B. Leonard, "The Future of Sex," *Look,* July 25, 1967.

. . . the whole importance of this insistence on land is just now beginning to be understood. Malcolm said many times that when you speak about revolution you're talking about land—changing the ownership or usership of some specific land which you think is yours. But any talk of Nationalism . . . which is not intent on restoring or securing autonomous space for a people, i.e., a nation, is at the very least shortsighted.[3]

Can we not ask the same question about Nationalism that we asked about the masculine role? Is the kind of nationalism that Jones is describing inclusive enough to be meaningful as a part of a larger nationalism? That is, isn't the real concern of the New Movement freedom from oppression within the white structure rather than freedom next to it? Moreover, does this kind of nationalism take into account the need for changes in the oppressing structures? In a sense, this kind of nationalism seems to embrace structures of the existing system, asking only that it be allowed to continue the same thing alongside it.

Perhaps we should consider in this context whether or not we should "allow" certain anachronistic attitudes on the part of the New Movement. Some have said "they" must go through this stage before "they" can arrive at a more "sophisticated" world view. Others say that this is the only possible posture left open to the oppressed Negro. He has been beaten down for so long and so completely that it is unrealistic to assume that he can magnanimously be concerned about anything but his own perseverance.

To assume that the Black Nationalist movement in the United States must go through a stage of nationalism assumes that progress only moves through certain predetermined steps.

[3] LeRoi Jones, "The Legacy of Malcolm X, and the Coming of the Black Nation," *Home: Social Essays* (William Morrow and Co., New York, 1966), pp. 241-242.

Before a group or nation can reach a certain plateau of development, it must go through necessary stages of development. Such theories of history find more exceptions to their rules than "proofs." Furthermore, a theory of history which assumes developmental stages is highly questionable vis-à-vis a nation's posture toward other nations. There is little evidence to show that this nation's foreign policy has moved from a highly isolationist nationalism of the nineteenth century to a more responsible "internationalism" because it has worked through its developmental tasks. The technological revolution has so radically changed the limits and nature of war that an "enlightened" self-interest makes isolationism impossible. Thus, it is more likely out of motives of self-preservation and not from a process of maturation that a nation's posture toward the rest of the world changes.

Some have said that the troubles we are seeing in our cities these days are but the symptom of an adolescent stage of rebellion against an overpaternalistic society. From adolescent rebellion the black man will move to a more mature position. It seems that we will allow the kids to have their fling while we understandably stand by, waiting for them to wake up to the fact of their juvenile behavior and take their proper places in society. It's the kind of thing I have heard so often: "I felt that way when I was a boy, Sonny; you'll have a different perspective when you're older." This is paternalism par excellence. Is it necessary to assume that action between groups or individuals can only begin in terms of rebellion before growing to maturity? Is it not possible that action can be in terms of equity without going through an adolescent stage?

A large part of the problem of American Black Nationalism seems to be that it is very much caught up and trapped in its own rhetoric. It may be that the black man in America is seeing his African brothers emerging from the control of ab-

sentee colonialists and assumes that the two situations are
parallel. Indeed, there are many parallels, but there is a tendency to get hung up on the rhetoric of nationalism which
skews the verbalization of the concern for becoming a part of
this white nation. Even Carmichael tacitly admits this when
he says:

They [the establishment] don't want to face the real problem
which is a man is poor for one reason and one reason only:
because he does not have money. If you want to get rid of poverty,
you give people money, period. . . . So the question then clearly is
not whether or not one can work, it is who has power. Who has
power to make his or her acts legitimate. That is all. And in this
country that power is invested in the hands of white people and
they make their acts legitimate.

Carmichael is not pointing to the setting up of a separate
nation, a separate land, a separate economy. He is asking for
the ability to participate in the nation which has not heretofore let him participate. And if the New Movement is going to
have the ability to participate, it does not necessarily have to
first assume the stance of nationalism. Such a stance may be
adequate for a country where the majority is oppressed and
the ruling minority is being thrown out, but we are in quite a
different situation in the United States. Separatism can only
give ego satisfaction to the oppressed; it will not be adequate
for a revolution which seeks to make a place for the oppressed
in the majority culture.

Another question which must be asked of the Black Power
movement has to do with the problem of power itself. A case
can be made for the fact that the New Movement does not yet
really believe in power, particularly in the North. Power is

seen in deed and is thought to be merely a disruptive force, and there is little to make one sense that the leaders of the Movement believe that power can be channeled, controlled, and used for certain specific ends. In the South this is less true than in the North. The Black Panther Party has been able to gain power and use it for the ends of the Movement. But in the North little has been done which would show that black men really believe that they can develop power and use it to shape the kind of a world in which they want to live. Where have been those who have gained power in the black community? They have lost sight of the goals for which they were going to use the power. They are either awestruck by the massiveness of the power over against them, or they are corrupted by their new power and use it only for their own self-glorification.

Finally, the New Movement has gotten itself in the box of allowing its antipaternalism to become antiwhiteism. The Movement has lost the ability to form alliances and to use those that it can to achieve its own ends. Not even Malcolm X was this myopic:

. . . we nationalists used to think we were militant. We were just dogmatic. It didn't bring us anything.

Now I know it's smarter to say you're going to shoot a man for what he is doing to you than because he is white. If you attack him because he is white, you give him no out. He can't stop being white. We've got to give the man a chance. He probably won't take it, the snake. But we've got to give him a chance.

We've got to be more flexible. Why, when some of our friends in Africa didn't know how to do things, they went ahead and called in some German technicians. And they had blue eyes.

I'm not going to be in anybody's straitjacket. I don't care what a

person looks like or where they come from. My mind is wide open
to anybody who will help get the ape off our backs.[4]

This brings us to the question of how the Churches of the
major Protestant denominations, which are indeed white
middle-class institutions, are going to minister to a black community which has clearly pointed out the failures and demonic
elements of those Churches? Indeed, how can the Church minister in a place where it is not only unwanted, but is openly
and actively despised? Is there a place for the white missionary
in the black ghettos of our land?

Is it possible for the Church in its proclamation and structure to affirm Black Power and deny its misuses? Is it possible
for a white institution or ministry to deny paternalism and by
its word and action affirm, encourage, and foster self-
determination? Can the Church affirm the need for black
symbolism, history, and culture, and effectively deny black
racism as well as white racism? Is it possible for a white institution to minister in a black community?

These questions push at the white Church and almost seem
to overwhelm its missionary possibility in the ghetto. It is the
thesis of this paper, however, to affirm a positive role for these
Churches in the ghetto. Indeed, each of these Churches cannot
abdicate its responsibility to be a proclaimer and an effective
institution for change in the black community—as well as the
white community—even though the Church's inadequacy in
both places is glaring.

With respect to the black community the white Church has
gotten itself into a position that—partly out of its guilt for
having been a part of the problem and partly out of its fear of

[4] Malcolm X, *Malcolm X Speaks: Selected Speeches and Statements,* ed.
by George Breitman (Grove Press, New York, 1966), p. 213.

not being liked, loved, and accepted by those it is seeking to reconcile to the gospel, which it is not quite sure is a saving gospel—it has been almost immobilized in carrying on the task that needs to be done. No matter how sophisticated we like to think we are in talking realistically about the problems of the world, almost all of us white do-gooders still have vestiges of believing that the style of Jesus was best proclaimed in Willie Loman's assumption that to be "successful" we need to be well-liked. We need to be confronted in this time of ours with the fact that not all the world is in the bag of the Athenians "who spent their time in nothing except telling or hearing something new" (Acts 17:21), but that there are many who are like those at Ephesus where "there arose no little stir concerning the Way" (Acts 19:23). Like Paul, on occasion it may be necessary for some of us to be let over the city walls in a basket, but our presence is called for among all groups and all peoples—even those who would rather see us dead. ("The only good honkie is a dead honkie.")

If we are going to affirm our belief in the task of reconciliation between races, there must be some white presence in the ghetto. If we are going to take seriously Paul's affirmation that in Christ there is neither Jew nor Greek, slave nor free, male nor female, there must be some form of witness on the part of the Church that separation leads away from fullness of life. The Church took its stand against "separate but equal" when this was the justification of white behavior; it should also take its stand against this understanding when it is the doctrine of the black man.

Here, clearly, is the task of the Church. In the first place the Church must listen. The Church must LISTEN. Carmichael, Karenga, McKissick, Elija Muhammed, Brown, each is absolutely accurate in his description of the failure of the Church.

We need to hear that. While these men have much to contribute concerning the need for power, the debilitating effects of paternalism, etc., they need to be confronted with the inadequacy of their Neo-Puritanism, their shortsighted disruptiveness, and their racism. The Church must be called to repentance for what it has done and is doing to the blacks; it must be called to renewal for what it should be doing in black and white communities alike, and it must be called to speak the word of judgment even against those it has oppressed and about whom it is now, rightly, guilty as hell.

For the Church to undertake these tasks in the black communities, it must take seriously the task of being first and foremost the Church. That is, those missions that we have in the ghetto must not become merely apologists for the Black Power movement or agents of the Federal Government through the War on Poverty. And it is not merely enough for the Church to stand "in between" the factions: one faction which wants order at the price of justice and the other which wants justice at the price of order. The role of the Church is and must be that of proclaimer and enabler for both groups. In the ghetto, in the suburbs, and in the political capitals the Church must listen, proclaim, and use its untapped power (political and economic) to free the blacks. In order to undertake these varied tasks the Church must take varied forms in each particular situation. Let us now suggest four aspects or forms of ministry that the Church must undertake in the ghetto.

The first facet or aspect of the Church's ministry in the ghetto must be celebration. And by celebration we mean here not only all those very sophisticated meanings of the word that the Church Fathers have delineated for us, but we also mean the unadulterated excitement and joy that people can have about their presence together and their common freeing faith.

What an atrocity it has been that in so many mission Churches our missionaries have done all in their power to stifle the tradition of exuberance of the black Christian Churches. How many missions have we seen where the ministry has done all in its power to prevent the message of joy from being heard joyously? The good news is virtually smothered by the media of drab hymns, drab liturgy, and drab preaching.

The celebration of the Church in the ghetto needs to pick up those aspects of the tradition of the community to which it is ministering, the aspects that can be affirmed with integrity, and the Church must affirm them. This task is not easily done by whites steeped in a tradition of dour American Gothic Puritanism. The celebrational life of the ghetto Church can only authentically and creatively be done by a black man. I say this not only because of the familiarity and ease with which he might move, using the traditions of his culture, but also for the symbolic purposes of black leadership. The leader of worship is highly visible and helps meet the clear and authentic need, as the nationalists have pointed out, for images of successful, authentic black leadership for the community to emulate. The development of images that blacks can pattern their lives after and which affirm their heritage, their potential, and their sense of worth should be the task of the Church.

The second aspect of the ghetto Church ministry must be education. Here we are speaking of a whole range of educational tasks which the schools are not now doing in the ghetto —from teaching the three R's to helping people become biblically literate, from focusing on the value questions of the postmodern era, including leisure, work, sexuality, the shape of the family, etc., to developing an adequate theological symbolism that will give intellectual constructs from which these people might reject the inadequacies of Fundamentalism and other limited world views. The task of education is a massive one; every ounce of resources that the Church has could be poured into it, and the job would only be begun. Nonetheless, it must be undertaken.

Those who are oppressed by the *kismet* doctrines of the storefront Churches must hear the freeing word of the gospel of the kingdom of God which is breaking into our world now. Those who are confused by the preaching of the nationalists must have tools to distinguish their legitimate prophecy from their demagoguery. Those who are not getting the intellectual skills from our school system, the skills that they need to compete in our society as it is, must be given the tools they need. Even though we cannot claim that we can begin to do the job that needs to be done, we must begin.

The paternalism of the Church in the past has been so pervasive that it has not allowed the Church to do the task we are called to do. Too often the assumption on the part of the Church has been that the people it is serving in the ghettos of this country are incapable of digesting the meat that they need to be fully human. So, only pabulum has been allowed in their diet. No wonder the mission Churches have been such failures in the production of leadership. Not until the Churches begin with the assumption that they are working with intellectual equals can they begin the real task of education or dialog.

In the third place, the Church must undertake the task of organization. Here Black Power speaks loud and clear. Powerless people will continue to be oppressed as long as they are not able to see to their own interests. It should not come as a shock to one that the human creature is still a sinful one, primarily concerned with his own self-interest. In such a world the powerless remain oppressed as long as they cannot or do not exercise their right to protect their own self-interest. Voter organization, welfare-rights organization, economic development, the initiation of small business, and the development of

P.T.A.'s and other special interest groups for the achievement of specific ends must be undertaken by the Church if it is to be something more than a "Do as I say, not as I do organization," which it already has been for far too long.

In this realm the Church could not only become a teacher but an example of the uses of power for specific, limited ends for the betterment of not only the oppressed but also the oppressor. As we mentioned above, the goals of the Black Power movement are not inclusive enough nor are they specific enough. Beyond that, most of the movement at this point is concerned with rhetoric and has little sense of tactics and strategy. If planned change is to come about, organizational methods must be learned and the opportunity to use them given to the people who know the need and the remedies that will fill the need. The ghettos are still lacking the skills needed to shape their own destiny, and the tools can and must be given to them to fulfill this task.

Finally, the ghetto Church's ministry must be a mission not only to the colonized but also to the colonizers. It is my feeling that there can be no serious efforts on behalf of the oppressed until the oppressors can see and smell the effects of their oppression. As long as the white middle-class Church is carefully isolated from what is happening in the inner city far from their suburban enclaves, the sense of urgency and need will only be academic. Opportunity must be made for the do-gooders of our country to know what is happening about them before they will really become concerned. This means that the ghetto Church not only should be an interpreter to the Churches outside but must also be an observation point from which the suburbanite might view the ruins about him. As onerous as the task is for many of us in the inner city of allowing those that we have often called tourists, and other pejorative terms it would not be well to mention here, to use the Churches of which we are a part as observation points, nonetheless, this kind of experience is more often than not invaluable in reorienting those who previously had little understanding and less concern.

We have not spoken here of the usual forms of Church life, where the word is preached and the sacraments administered, or which is the locus of *koinonia, diakonia,* and *kerygma.* We have tried to lift up the special problem that a mission Church has in an age of Black Power in the ghetto, specifically asking the question of the viability of a white ministry in a black community. We have tried to answer this question by affirming a good deal of what the Black Power movement is saying and incorporating this into what the shape of the Church in the ghetto might be. Particularly, black preaching is needed, but white missionaries and white resources can be used in the areas of education, organization, and interpretation. The leadership, however, must come from the black community itself. The posture of the ghetto Church should be one of directly confronting the issues of Black Power as well as the issues of poverty, powerlessness, and racial oppression. Until the Church can find such a posture, it will continue to be immobilized, like the frosting on a decaying cake.

14/ The Church:
Served or Serving

by NAOMI L. M. LONG

*"Strange thing about this Church deal," the young mother of a
family commented. "It always seems to be saying one thing to
you and demanding another thing of you. Our priest keeps
talking about the Christian virtues of the family and keeping
the family together, and yet what happens? He expects my
husband to attend the men's meeting one night a week, my
daughter to go to the youth group another night a week, my
son to belong to the boys' club another night, and me, not only
to be secretary of the Women's Guild but also to organize
the dinners we have to put on for various civic groups of the
town. Now he wants me to become the leader of a young girls'
group. When do we have the chance to practice being a family?"*

It was a private club with various subgroups—a total reflection of the small-town society as it existed, only the club happened to have a building, or a set of buildings, and it happened to be called St. Swithin's. And in suburbia the same
club with the same setup happened to be called Christ Church
or St. John's, and downtown it would be called the Cathedral
Church of St. Paul, and in the ghetto, St. Cyprian's or Grace
Church—little havens of spiritual comfort where one is told
how to salve one's conscience by using pious talk, by getting

rid of one's old clothes by giving them to worthy causes, and by placing an already-pledged amount of money in a collection plate regularly. And the leader, one's priest, sanctified by hundreds of years of traditional ceremony, will break the bread and pour the wine, so that, together with others of like community status one becomes a part of the body of this Church—this flock, the chosen ones. And when a stranger of like species appears, he is engulfed by the club. If he is not of like species, the members make sure that he goes somewhere else, or nowhere at all.

In 1958 I became an administrator in one of the subgroups of this private club called Church. It was the Episcopal Church, and its area was the Diocese of Michigan. The subgroup was the girls' organization. I came into the Church really believing that Christianity spoke to life—to blood brotherhood and soul sisterhood, to the equality of all persons, to the reality of unselfish love: the sharing of life, substance, and death with other human beings. I really believed that Christianity was the way that changes could be brought about among people in the various levels of society, changes which could break the stupidity of the world scene. I believed that Christ's teachings and life were the guidelines for life, no matter where we lived it, and that if these demanded change in attitude or behavior or both, then we made that change in our own lives and circumstances. I believed that the Church was the vehicle for carrying this out.

I really believed that others in this Church believed this too, and that this was what they were working toward. I believed that so-called success for the Church was not based on obvious material things like income, size of membership, and real estate, but on the extent to which actual life of the Church mirrored Christ's magnificent philosophy and life.

Through administration of the organization I gained an insight into the intricacies of deception that the Church had made of Christianity. The Church really has become a private club which exists in addition to life and does not involve life itself. It exists for the people who belong to it, and they make sure that it maintains the power to perpetuate itself.

Leadership is the key to any kind of organization. Through the leader the aims and objectives of the organization can be realized by its members. So, will not the aims of the youth organizations in the Church reflect what the Church wants them to be? Or at least what the adult leaders in the Church or the priests want them to be? And these leaders and priests do not trust the young people unless they are doing mere "busy work" in the Church. So the groups are composed of the young people who "fit in" with Church busyness. They are the small cliques which exist for a while, and then they fade out when the cliques disintegrate.

The aim and objective of most Church leaders is that the young people will become good Church members. In this respect they do not even admit that the children are already human beings and already a part of the Church, let alone being already Christian.

And the leaders of the subgroups play into the hands of the clergy, and the clergy play into the hands of the diocesan administration which is controlled by the bishop. And the measuring line for success is materialistic and tangible.

There was a young mother—one of the members of Christ Church, Episcopal. She lived in the area where her Church was located—a nice suburb of Detroit. Her husband and she had moved to this area so that their children would grow up in a "nice" area and have other "nice" children for friends. When she was young, Mrs. White had belonged to the Girls' Club in her own parish. Her rector knew this and knew that she had a daughter of the right age for one of these girls' groups. He wanted to have his beautiful new pseudo-Gothic educational buildings used more than just once a week. So he flattered Mrs. White by telling her that she was just the right person to run the parish Girls' Club since she had had experience with the Club in her own youth.

The membership consisted of Mrs. White's daughter's friends. She found much busy work for the girls to do. But when it came to leadership training seminars, it was always a problem for Mrs. White to attend. Her group rarely participated in interparochial-group activities because she did not like them to mix with other groups. And when her daughter grew old enough to belong to the co-ed youth group, the girls' group disintegrated. Some say the group fulfilled a need. What need?

And then Mrs. White came to a leadership training course given by the central diocesan administration. She found that several Negroes were attending it, and, because it was being held in a downtown Church, said that transportation was too difficult, and she quit.

At this same time, in another district in Detroit the rector of St. Thomas Church talked to the diocesan administration. "You know," he said, "we have had a girls' group here continuously for the past twenty years, but a couple of weeks ago the leader said she was quitting because all the children who were coming to join were colored children. However, I have found a very good Negro woman for a new leader. She does need some leadership training though, and I want her to come to your training sessions so that when the time is right in the parish we can have the admission service. When is your next course starting?"

The new course started. The new Negro leader was a participant. That was the course that Mrs. White started and quit.

St. Thomas' admission service took place about three

months later. The rector's little girl was the only white girl. He told me that he had questioned her about feeling obvious but it did not worry her. And although this young girls' group was all Negro, about ninety percent of the congregation was white. I recalled a remark of Dr. Martin Luther King: "The time of integration is during the changing of neighborhoods."

About forty miles out of Detroit is a little town. A new rector had just taken over the Episcopal parish. The involvement of family membership totaled about thirty at the most. The rector came to me as the administrative leader of the Episcopal Girls' Organization. "Most, if not all of my young people are girls, so I thought it would be good to get them involved in the girls' diocesan organization," he said. He was young and vigorous and wanted the Church to look alive, so they started on an extensive building program for a "good-looking" Church. He wanted to draw his people together on a tangible project because he felt this would mold them into a group. He was spurred on by the bishop who had been inciting the parishes into building programs because the big General Convention was coming to Detroit, and he wanted things to look vital. (If we merely work with people, there is no evidence that can be quickly assessed or measured by visitors or the administration. Yet to work with people is our commission or commitment as Christians.)

However, this nice clique of white girls became the girls' group in the Episcopal Church at Holly. Sometime later, and quite accidentally, I discovered that Negroes, too, formed a part of the population in Holly. None of the programs, whose aim and objective was to help the girls interpret Christianity in their lives not only at home but also in the community and which they participated in, touched their conscience. And the Church itself, with its elaborate programs of human relations, was swallowed up in the ocean of tangible real estate.

At St. Alfred's Church the rector phoned me about these girls' groups. "I have a leader for our girls. She is having some difficulties in her relationships with other people and really needs an outlet of some kind. I think that the responsibility of a group of girls will help her get away from her introverted thinking and enable her to behave more rationally." So this group of girls was at the mercy of a dominating and dictating female.

We held leadership training conferences in various Church groupings or convocations, and I discovered that the convocations were designed so that white Churches stayed in their own areas. But if the arrangement was for them to come downtown or into the ghetto of the city, they had such transportation difficulties that they could not make it. The Negro Churches in the ghetto would invite them to a function, and they would come warily, have a good time for a short while, and then drive back into the ghetto of suburbia. And it was all done with the busyness of subdivision and suburban living determining their behavior. The call of human equality, and the dignity that accompanies it, had no real affect upon their choices. The underlying truths were never stated by either side—black or white, ghetto or suburbia, the gutter or the castle.

The Christian brotherhood bit and human relationship bit are constantly projected in conferences; they get a good deal of attention at the conference table. "We go round and round the point for a whole day," someone remarked once, "and then at the last minute, when there is no time left to deal with the question, we are left with the hot potato of interracial marriage in our hands, never resolved." Yet, this is the starting point of human relations. Why should race or color or creed have anything to do with this?

Negro children are aware of who they are, where they live,

and why they live there at a very early age. If this is so, why cannot the young subgroups in the Church allow all their young people to become aware of the same thing? Simply because these little cliquey Church groups exist to protect their young people from the inroads of the outside community.

"We are having difficulty with one girl in our group," one leader confided to me. *"She comes from the housing settlement which is on the boundary of our area. But she is different from the rest of the girls and is bringing into the group quite a disturbing element. I am hoping that she will soon 'fit in' with the other girls."* And so began the brainwashing techniques and the techniques of gradually getting rid of this "alien" element—the disdainful looks because she is not dressed the same, the remarks *"Aren't you glad you are not like her?"* and the "I-am-better-than-thou" attitude.

"I want to form a girls' group at the Church," one woman said to me, *"because my daughter is old enough to belong to a club, and I want her to have a safe club to belong to until she is old enough to be safe in a co-ed youth group."* This damnable word *"safe"* increasingly irritates like an ingrowing toenail. And even Negro leaders in Churches in the ghetto wanted safe clubs for their children, for their youth, for themselves. Is this why Churches are locked and why the rectors live in suburbia and keep office hours?

Again it is the noninvolvement of this private club called "Church" in life itself which began to press upon my development of programs which would force involvement. The conference table, the summer camp—these were the immediate media. Both of these had the sincere approval of the central administration. Indeed, great statements and good publicity come from conferences, and as a result the administration can remark, "See—black and white sit down together, participate in communion together, and make significant statements which can change the world." And at the end of the conference, the participants get into their cars and drive back to their small towns, their suburban ranch homes, their houses in the subdivision and the ghetto. If their ideas have been aired, if their attitudes have been partially changed, if new friendships have been formed, what difference does it make because all go back into their snail-shell living once again? Although they have *said* something, nothing will actually be *done*.

"I want my girl to attend your summer camp this year," one mother said to me, "because this is her only chance of coming in contact with Negroes." At first this made me believe that we were accomplishing something. But she only stayed for two weeks, and what are two weeks out of a lifetime?

A member of the camp committee asked at one of the meetings, "How many colored children were at camp this summer?" "I really have no idea," I replied, "I could probably get some idea by going through registration forms and checking the parishes the girls came from and their addresses." "Oh, don't bother. But I heard that there were a lot of colored girls in camp, and I would not like to think there might be just one white girl in a group by herself with all the others colored. It would be a difficult situation for her." I could only reply "That is what you have expected of Negro children for over a hundred years." She changed the subject of conversation.

Then I began to see that conferences were the easy way out. Summer camp was the easy way out. It surely is quite possible that a human being, professing Christianity and belonging to the Church, this private institution or club, can live in a way other than she speaks. We can confess our sins on Sundays, have bread broken for us and wine poured for us, and receive a so-called absolution without anything happening. The white Churches remain white Churches, and the Negro Churches remain Negro, and the bishop hears the statements from joint conferences and says, "The Church has its doors open to everyone. Hear the great things we are saying." And Jesus Christ gets hidden in a closet, with not even a skeleton remaining to fall out of the door when it is accidentally opened.

Then, even though I believed that changes could come through the young people, I forgot that young people are merely the reflection of their parents and the society in which they live. And as far as this Episcopal Church bit goes, it exists in a secure society. Who wants to give away security? It is only those who have nothing to lose who are willing to fight for something which may be better. When people have security and an abundance of material things, even if they are all on credit, they do not want to lose them, and they would be prepared to fight to retain them against anyone who would take them away. And the children pick up this attitude from their parents.

Listen to this fourteen-year-old girl from Grosse Pointe: "What does all this Jesus stuff mean—give away everything you have and live? Share what you have with everyone else? He who loses his life will find it? I don't understand it. How can I give away what my parents give me? My friends accept me because of what I have—the clothes I wear, the car I drive, or will be driving, the place I live. I can't give these things away. So what? I can't go along with what Jesus says."

And neither can the Church, because she has become sidetracked into the private-club deal with all the real estate and the yearly budgets and the rotating administration composed of people with the right addresses. And for a diocesan administration of a subgroup of the Church with a pet project, the right address is Grosse Pointe or Birmingham or Bloomfield Hills or Rochester. And who was I to think any change could come even for Christ's sake?

This club with its ivy-covered Gothic and pseudo-Gothic architecture began to close in on me because it made no changes in life. Little girls were getting killed in Sunday school in the south, and the Church did not say a word. Bussed-in Negro children were being turned away from certain public schools in Detroit, and the Church didn't say a word. A white priest at an Episcopal Church in Detroit gave four little Negro girls their bus fare to a Negro Church, instead of letting them come to his Church. In our own girls' organization certain branches never came to total group activities, or if they came, they left very early because more Negroes than whites were there. But it was too subtle for outright warfare—because we were a part of the Church, this magical thing of equality and brotherhood, which were talked and never lived.

Program was the dominant word. What is the program of your organization? What is the program of the Church? An organization, a private club, an institution can develop a program.

I became involved in a drop-in center in a storefront on Mack Avenue on Eastside Detroit for the students from Eastern High School. This had been established after much conferencing with the clergy and youth workers from this area. Those of us involved in setting up the center were adults— some were clergy, some were youth workers, and some were just concerned citizens. They were concerned about the teenage wanderers, and the insidious fact that none of us lived in the area made each one of us try to work out what our "program" should be.

I discovered that when we start to think about "program," we give the lie to the fact that we are trying to do something *for* people. This is not life. If we wanted to get to know these young people, why not live there?

One young college student came to work with us. He said,

"My parents would disown me if they knew I was working among these people and in this area. I've just realized these boys all carry knives and every time I walk in here I expect to be knifed on the way."

And yet this same student gained a tremendous sense of living when he was able to relax with the local young people who came dribbling in from the street. He found that he could talk naturally with them. And all the time our older staff wanted to have a program—"What are we going to *do* with these young people?" A couple of blocks down the street was another storefront where a group of young people used to gather. But they gathered after they had been sitting on the stoops of the disintegrating houses where the local kids lived, talking with them, being with them. And their program naturally evolved from their acquaintance with the kids, with the local people, simply because they sat and *were* long enough to hear and experience. Then, from this came a sharing of experience: first, in trying to demonstrate that indeed police brutality did exist and, second, in proving that racial discrimination also existed in the businesses in the area.

Our center gave moral support, but never became involved because the "Church" always stands for law and order, and what is more, funds might have been cut off if we deviated from our "program." Therefore, just like the Church, we sat in our little ivory-tower storefront while the meat of living life got mangled on the chopping block of the legal power-structure.

It was at this point that I could no longer sit behind a desk and think up elaborate programs for people, no matter who they were. I was living a lie. Jesus Christ never sat behind a desk and worked out an involved program. He went out and lived with people. All his fights were with the religious leaders, the bulwarks of the synagogue, the private club in his time.

They were eventually to destroy him because he had lived with and had enabled degraded persons to gain dignity. And I needed to find people and live with them, to share and work with them.

Letter to an Australian friend, June, 1965:

"... *It is so strange. I am not finding the future working out in the fields I am confident about. I am taking life, or trying to take it, by looking at it as objectively as I can. And I am finding that when one begins to live on the peoples' level, and the very bottom at that, the person I had developed into doesn't apply here in Mississippi—a place where life is raw, at rock bottom, depressed by a white power-structure which I unwittingly represent.*

"... *I am finding more and more that the Church as such doesn't belong in this life, and I am speaking of the Church as the institution, the private club, the Establishment, the bit that it is in peoples' lives and the fraud that it has become—its false values, its tie-up with white middle-class religion of material things and family, etc. Christianity has a place, but it is life and not religion, or Church, or anything except life in its rawness, in its nothingness, in its basic values, in its relationships, in its communication of person to person—and the Church has nothing to do with these things.*

"... *I am finding this because I have left behind what I had. I could be living relatively comfortably in Detroit, being thought a lot of, feeling important in an administrative position, going away for a vacation every now and again, having a dog, seeing good shows when I want to, etc.*

"... *During the past few weeks I have been through some devastating moral decisions. I don't know their rightness, but as Malcolm once said, 'One does not have to question motivation or tear oneself apart examining motives when one is committed.' This is alright as long as one knows one's commit-*

ment. Basically, it is still trying to find out where Christ fits in life, and I am coming to find that this can only come in a huge upheaval of society because one section of it cannot, in any shape or form, take the other side of it. And it is in the meeting of the two that Christianity gets worked out. But within this concept, the Church, as such, does not exist. Thus the integrating of Churches becomes totally unimportant in this struggle, I feel. Mississippi, to outside whites, would seem to be a most religious state—a high percentage of churchgoing, religious sessions on the radio all the time, revival meetings all over the place, but all the time just the old bible stuff. The Churches are entirely missing out on the vital living questions and all the civil rights challenges; indeed the Churches denounce these for being Communist in nature and principle. . . ."

"How do you get along with white people in Mississippi?"

"I really don't know. I don't know any, except of course some civil rights workers who are still there and some of the National Council of Churches workers—but they are not a part of the Mississippi white social-structure."

There was no way of getting to know any of the white people when you were working with Negroes.

"Well, isn't the National Council of Churches supposed to be carrying out a program of reconciliation?"

"What do you mean by that? Reconciliation on whose part?"

Here again we find in the institution people looking for program—what are we doing *for* somebody else so that they might become like us, nice little stamped-out copies of our designing? And by "our" I mean the white power-structure. And the Church in Mississippi is a part of this structure. And it represents so-called law and order. The summer of 1964 seemed to be a time of awakening on the part of many people.

One middle-aged lady from a tiny town in a rural Delta county said, "My eyes were opened that summer. This young fellow sat and talked with us about our situation. I didn't know there was anything different. I've always lived in this little shack and have never made any more than ten dollars a week working in the field. But he told us about something called minimum wages, and he told us about voting and how we could get to vote, and he told us there was a better life that we should be able to live. And I haven't worked in that field since, and I will fight the white man for what has been and is mine. And I will go on fighting in the Movement even if I die in it."

About fifty persons—white and Negro—were in the abandoned Air Force Base, still owned by the Federal Government, in Greenville, Mississippi. There were there to demonstrate to the authorities the urgency of releasing twenty-four million dollars worth of surplus food donated by the Federal Department of Agriculture to the poor people of Mississippi. The Office of Economic Opportunity had promised one and a quarter million dollars for wages for the poor people who were to distribute the food. The state authorities had held all this up because they wanted it distributed their way, which, of course, followed the stereotyped white power-structure method. We were ordered to leave or we would be thrown out. We stayed.

After several meetings someone in the group came up with some prayer-meeting songs. Old, grey-haired Mrs. Carnegie turned stolidly to one of the windows, "Now isn't the time to be crying out to God. We don't need religion now, we need action and strength in ourselves. Let's quit this flying to God for everything." She had been in jail the year before for demonstrating against the white power-structure with many others. She had spent ten days sitting on a concrete floor of a building at the Fairground because the jail was not big enough for everybody, and she had been kicked by the police because she could not get up quickly from the concrete. She knew the fallacy of the brainwashed Negro religion, and she had found strength in the dignity of the fight for freedom from white domination.

A group of young Mississippi Freedom Corps workers attended a Church service in Edwards, a small town near Jackson, Mississippi. They wore clean clothes, even though they were not "Sunday suits." The local pastor proceeded to preach about being bathed and properly clothed to come to Church—preached that they must wear suits and use deodorant, that being clean was godliness. Four of these young fellows and two of the girls had been thrown out of school the year before for participating in demonstrations for their human dignity; two of them later helped a starving family get off a plantation, and the plantation owner fired at the truck as they left. One of them could not go home because the owner of his mother's shack was white and had found out that the young man had participated in civil rights activity. And yet this religion, brainwashed by the white Church, was dictating salvation in terms of clean clothes.

A program of reconciliation? Reconciliation to what? On whose terms? By what standards?

A Mississippi white lawyer, supposedly "liberal," told a meeting of the Delta Ministry of the National Council of Churches how the Negro could crack the white power-structure: "Bring economic pressure to bear on the white and you could squeeze him out." Then he added "But you must not do it. You cannot do it."

When a person realizes his dignity as a human being, he cannot relinquish it again to oppression. He must fight to maintain it, even if he is destroyed in the fight. Dignity is the beginning of freedom, and freedom concerns the dignity of others. We find each other by how we live and by how we care about each other.

The reality of love comes by overstepping the boundaries which keep us in social, economic, and racial ghettos.

Love can exist only as it is tested, and this testing involves action, and action involves life . . . life itself. Therefore, is not love demonstrated in the involvement of person with person as the battle for human-ness is played out in the arena of discrimination?

And is not a private club a form of discrimination—if rules and regulations are set up for its existence and perpetuation, whether these rules are stated or not? Is the Church then another form of discrimination? Is the real Church then underground? Unseen, but found among those who seek to free others *from* discrimination and oppression of human-ness? And is not the Church found by demonstrating what real love can be in life?

15/ The World, My Church; My Life, My Prayer

by SHARON MURDOCH

"IF I WERE GOD. . . ."

It was undoubtedly the most fantastic contest ever conceived. Harry could hardly believe his eyes when he read it. But here it was—right in a national magazine. Something you always dreamed about, but never really dared hope for—until now. No money as grand prize—and there was only one prize, no second or third—no yacht, car, or fabulous home, not even a color T.V. or your very own plane. But the prize. . . .

Harry grabbed a pen from his cluttered desk and armed himself with paper. "Now, in twenty-five words or less, 'I want to be God for a Day because. . . .' Well, why do I want to be God?" Harry asked himself. "Something the judges will like."

Hours later Harry threw down his unused pen with a little cry of "Help!" *"That's it!* That's why I want to be God—so I can help people. Only more than I can now." He remembered back when he had been a child in Milwaukee. He had been playing in his yard one evening when it was just getting dark, and this old wrinkly woman had come along and fallen on the sidewalk. She cried, "Somebody help me," and as Harry ran out the gate, he saw that she had fallen on one of his skates that had rolled under the fence and onto the sidewalk.

193

But because the woman was very old, she died as Harry bent over to help her.

"Yes, I want to help people." Harry carefully worded his entry, then just as carefully wrote it out on the entry blank. Hmmm, not even any box tops or labels to enclose, thought Harry, as he deposited his letter in the mail box.

"Here Harry, have another drink! Excited? It should be a hell of a lark. If you want somebody else to take your place, old man, remember your ole buddy Bernie."

It just couldn't be real. He—Harry Richards—had won the contest! This was his going-away party, for tomorrow was the big day. Tomorrow, all day, he would be God.

"Why me?" wondered Harry. "I'm just an average guy. I like my job, even though the boss and I have our days. Nine to five aren't bad hours. I have a nice bachelor's apartment and pay my rent on time. I may drink a little too much at parties, but everyone is entitled to one or two; I mean it isn't as if I were an alcoholic or anything. Nothing exciting has ever happened to me. Well, except when my landlady's dog, Virginia Woolf, bit me. I'm not afraid of the dog, just wary. I wonder why the judges chose me? I guess that nobody else wanted to help other people—just themselves." Harry was very scornful of people like that, people who thought only of personal gain.

"This isn't at all what I was expecting," fretted Harry. Only five hours of the twenty-four had passed, and God-For-A-Day-Harry was upset. It wasn't the lark he'd expected; here he was floating on golden clouds, surrounded by beautiful angels, and helping fortune to smile at his friends, and while not exactly doing evil to "un-friends," he let them know. . . . Well, things just didn't go well for them that day.

These were childish fancies, and Harry was unhappy. He

was God, but he hadn't smiled all day. As God, he had to make "rounds" like a doctor. He saw people dying from horrible and frightening diseases that he had not even known existed. He saw men kill other men without mercy or compassion. Without even flinching. Oh, not kill, like with a gun— but by what they did, said, and were. And the children. Oh, the children were the worst, with their big eyes and their terrible need to be loved. They would grow up just like their parents: deceptive, hating, and loving only themselves. If only he could help to save them from this! Through love he would protect them.

For the first time Harry really saw people naked—for what they were. He saw their need to get rich quick, their false idols, and their hypocrisy. He saw the way men saw God, as a kind of Superman, a perfect being, willing to wink at times to avoid seeing what man did not desire him to see. Harry longed to tell them, to show them Truth. If only he could arouse within them compassion for each other, as well as for themselves.

And all the long day Harry did not smile. He wanted to go home. This was all a farce, and he was tired. He didn't want to see any more pain, suffering, and death. The burden he bore was already very heavy. He just wanted to go home and sit in his big green chair and have a beer and watch the football game on T.V.

Twenty-three hours and fifty minutes gone by. In ten minutes God would be just ordinary Harry Richards, and Harry could go home. In the morning he would go to the office and. . . .

There was a noise. It was terrible. It was . . . well, there was something about it that drew you to it. But it was such a hopeless noise. God-For-A-Day-Harry peered down through the clouds and looked over the lands. Then, in a large city he located the noise. Down a street in a poor section of town, in an overcrowded tenement building was a small child. A little girl in her room alone. Her father was lying drunk in the gutter two streets away. Her mother was working the "night shift," walking the lonely, and the not-so-lonely, streets. Tears streamed down the child's face, and she cried as if her little heart would break. "Give me strength," she prayed. "Please, somebody help me."

Perhaps the day was not a loss after all, thought Harry, remembering his entry for the "I want to be God for a Day because . . ." contest. God-For-A-Day-Harry turned gently and looked again at the lonely child; then a noise filled the heavens and space. It was soft at first, then grew louder and louder as Harry Richards laughed.

THE CHURCH IS PEOPLE

Unfortunately, I think that Harry is somewhat typical of many Church members today. He is an average man, really, the kind you might meet on the street, or know, or be. The "Harrys" sincerely want to help in any sort of way possible, but just cannot bring themselves to face the very real threat of giving themselves. To do this would make them too vulnerable. They can see what needs to be done, but too often just can't or won't do it. To these people, the word "Church" is not referring to a way of life, of living, but merely an accepted part of a routine, taken for granted, and demanding from them, at most, one hour a day once a week and ten percent of their income.

What comes to your mind when you hear the word "Church"? Perhaps you immediately think of that building in which you worship every Sunday morning, and you smile as you think of all the things that you love about that church: the beautiful altar linens and hangings, the vividly colored stained-glass windows, the hugh pipe organ it took several years to pay for, and the choir singing the hymns you've known since your youth. You love the service and know it by heart. Here, in this building, you find peace from the screaming headlines of the morning newspaper, with its count of the dead in Vietnam. Here, too, you find sanctuary from the cries of people, suppressed by hatred, prejudice, and bigotry, who riot in the streets of cities across the nation that their cause might be heard. There is quietness and serenity, not millions of people starving to death in India and China, not cold bitter facts of life, but peace, so that you might pray to God about the terrible situations which exist in the world today, such as poverty, war, and racism. This, to you, is "Church" as it is, and as it ought to be.

Or perhaps "Church" to you is a "covenanting community," a specific group of adults, bound together in covenant and following an established way of worship. Or maybe it's a list of rules which must be followed in order to gain salvation, or possibly it has no real meaning at all for you.

However, as I have grown up, questioned, and formed opinions, I have become more and more involved in the Church, and find myself not identified so much with a building or a certain stand on Church doctrine as with people. People and the world are my Church—not buildings, doctrines, services, but *people*. Just plain, ordinary, everyday people.

For the last two summers I have worked as a Volunteer in a poverty program in Wise County, Virginia, a part of the coal mining region of the state and of Appalachia, one of the primary targets of the War on Poverty. This area was once a great boom area, and the towns were wild and ahead of the game. Now, most of the mines have shut down, and there is no work. Coal had been the only industry, and even the poorest

could eke out a living from working in the mines. Now that is
gone, but the people remain, abandoned and forgotten and
poor, as the old mines now are. Although I worked primarily
with preschool mountain children in the Head Start program,
a large part of my job was to visit in the homes of my children,
getting to understand the mountain culture, and talking to the
parents about education and other concerns. As the program
progressed and I became increasingly involved in the lives of
the people with whom I was working, I discovered that I had
an overriding feeling of *being* the Church at work in the
world.

Back in college, I got into a discussion one evening with
one of my professors who maintained that the Church is a
dying institution, for its symbols are becoming obsolete and it
is no longer relevant. He saw the Church as a kind of club,
and maintained that other groupings could offer the same social opportunities and still demand as little as the Church. This
kind of a Church may be dying; in fact, I think that in many
ways it is already dead. But in its place is coming a new kind
of Church, which is relevant and cannot be otherwise. You
see, I am a part of this Church, and I and several hundred
thousand other people, many of them college age, are very
much *alive*. As a living part of this Church I am involved in
the lives of the people in Appalachia and all over. Had the
whole summer passed without my mentioning the word
"Church" to any of my mountain folk, the Church would still
have been relevant—because I was. As I was relating to them,
so too, was the Church.

So I see the Church of tomorrow as truly a Spirit-filled
community; I see it not as a building or glorified club, but as a
group of persons deeply committed to life and people and
working under the guidance of the Holy Spirit. This deep-
rooted concern for people necessarily involves this "new"

Church, sometimes radically, in the major issues of today: questions on Vietnam, the race issue, poverty—*people*.

There are many members of this "new" Church, and they come from all walks of life, all faiths. It is an ecumenical movement which is overtaking the old, established norm of differing denominations, each believing that its way is the "right" way. This movement recognizes that no one way can be right and concerns itself, not with quibbling over details, but with the very here-and-now need of people. They are aware that, as Bonhoeffer says, "to be a Christian is to participate in the suffering of God in the world." And there *is* suffering.

It may be difficult for the average person to imagine what it is like to live in the rural poverty areas, such as Wise. When one is surrounded by comforts, such as stereos and color television, and plenty of food, it is hard to believe that there can be such miserable poverty, but, unfortunately, it's true. One has only to travel as far as a slum neighborhood to find it.

Or go to Wise County, Virginia, population 43,579 in 1965. Here, the median income is $3,450, which is slightly better than the income of the families I was involved with, whose average income was $2,500 a year for a family of seven. Of the families there, 44.8% have annual incomes of less than $3,000. When one stops to consider the hard reality of these figures, it begins to make an impression. Compare these figures to your own family income. One can see why I just can't help but be bitter when Congress votes itself another one hundred percent raise in pay.

You know, it's easy to say, "Well, why don't they get out of there and get a job somewhere and do something?" without really understanding what holds these people captive. In order to comprehend, one must understand their whole culture. These people are tied to their homes by family and kin. They live from one check to the next, going further and further into debt, never being able to get very far ahead. Many are on welfare or social security and get food stamps, but these are rarely enough. Those who are able to scrape and save enough money to get to the "big city" to look for work there find themselves alone and unqualified for anything that would pay enough money to make sending for their families and trying to make a go of it worthwhile. They haven't enough education to get a decent paying job, and they don't have enough money to quit day work and go back to school. And so they return to the mountains, to family and kin, to the welfare checks, to the monotony. They are captives tangled in the web of poverty.

When I first went to Wise County for the program, we were told that the typical home we would be visiting would be two rooms and a path, but we never really believed it until we got down to visiting the families of our children. Then we came to realize that this was a world completely apart from any we'd known. If one were to ask one of these people if he wouldn't rather live in a colonial or a brick split-level, I'm sure he'd get a blank stare. For the most part, my children lived in combination wood and tar-paper buildings. There was rarely glass in the windows, but instead plastic, such as dry cleaning would be returned in. And there was always the path to the outhouse in back.

Inside the house might be wallpaper or paint depending on the type of walls and whether the family had enough money for it. A minimum of three children would sleep in a double bed, and two, in a single. In the kitchen would be an old coal stove where the cornbread and potatoes—the usual diet— were fixed, and in the living room, the television and a potbellied stove for warmth in the winter. It's easy for an outsider to criticize these people for owning television sets, when they don't have running water, but one must realize what a television set means to them. Many of the men do not have jobs, having been injured in the mines or in other mishaps, or just not having been able to find work; but whatever these people lack, seventy-six percent of them do have a television set. To these people, who will go way over their heads in debt to own one, a TV is their whole contact with the outside world. They are born, live, and will die probably within a one-hundred-mile radius of their place of birth. Many of them are living back in remote "hollers" in the mountains and rarely, if ever, see strangers.

It's difficult to try to describe the magnetic appeal of a TV to these people. It is at once a friend, a means of social experience and of information, and it is also a means of identification. Probably the most important reason, though, is that it is a means of escape. Here they can identify with a world completely different from the day-in and day-out monotony of their lives. There is a certain glamour on the television screen, and for a while these people aren't just a Mullins or a Boggs on Cricket Creek, but persons other people admire and respect and might want to be themselves.

The front porch has similar appeal. At any one time, driving down a country road, one can count a large number of people just sitting on the porch. This happens all the time, and I could never understand it until once I spent the weekend at the home of one of my children. The child's mother, a widow with eight children to raise, was on the verge of a nervous breakdown, so two other Volunteers and I took over "being mother" so that she could get away for a while for a much needed rest. Well, anyone who has ever tried to watch eight kids at once knows just what kind of a day we had; anyone who hasn't, should try to imagine the worst, and it was worse than that. The next morning though, after the children had been fed, I found myself drawn to the front porch, and there I experienced a very strange feeling. I looked out over the mountains and thought how beautiful they were, and as I watched, cars began to drive by on the way to town. It seemed as if I were watching the world go by. Suddenly the house and children, the exhaustion of the day before, and all my problems seemed very distant, if not nonexistent. It was as if, sitting in the cool, red glow of the morning, I had entered some state of euphoria, and no worldly thing could touch me. I sat there for at least an hour with kids climbing all over me, and I knew that I loved them deeply, even if they did seem like monsters at times, and I was glad to see that the "completely exhausted and drained feeling" was gone. An escape? Yes, certainly. But also there came some kind of inner strength to go on. Call it what you will—I call it the Holy Spirit working in my life.

In this day of higher education for almost anyone who wants it, it is difficult to believe that in this county only two percent of the people are college graduates. One cannot present a valid argument against programs such as Head Start when one realizes that here the median education is 7.3 grades, and that *twenty-five percent* of the people have less than five years of school. Having always taken my own college education for granted, I was shocked to learn that several of the parents of my children had *no* education whatsoever— they had never been to school! This isn't a thing to be very proud of in the twentieth century—with the scientific and technical knowledge we have gained. Americans can sympathize with backward, underdeveloped countries, but the same thing exists in this country, and I believe that this situation *must* be changed. I'm really baffled wondering *how* it could have happened in the first place, and *why* more isn't being done to combat this situation.

One cannot doubt the good of a program like Head Start

when one sees a child stand in wonder and awe with his hands under water running from a faucet, because the water at his house is hauled from a stream at the bottom of the "holler" in a bucket; or when one watches a child flush the toilet twenty-five times because it's not something familiar. One cannot help but feel pride and a sense of accomplishment when a child who hasn't spoken a single word for seven and one-half weeks —even when you loved him and reassured him and built his trust every day—finally begins to talk freely and openly. Where would these children have been without the socialization experience offered by the program, without the love offered by the Volunteers?

Where is the Church in these situations? Many *Churches* send old, used clothing to poverty areas as a salve for their own consciences. But they are not really out there doing anything about correcting the situation. Sending clothes, while it alleviates an immediate problem, doesn't help much in the long run. An old Chinese proverb says, "Give a man a fish and you feed him for one day, teach him *how* to fish and you feed him for a lifetime." This is what the "new" Church is trying to do. It's in there fighting, participating in the suffering, feeling the pain—living within it, and it within them. It's not afraid to get its hands "dirty" working with the desperate and trying to right a wrong. This is one of my big gripes with devotees of the institutional Church. It's as if getting dirty hands would really ruin them. At the end of the first summer's program, one of the local clergy asked for a list of things to be done on which the parish could follow through. At first I didn't give him any list because I didn't think that the parish would *want* to get involved. And if any member did it out of obligation, not wanting to, then he really wouldn't be giving any of himself anyway. Finally, after quite a bit of deliberation, I wrote the pastor telling him of one of my children.

This little girl was a doll and one of my very favorites. She was the kind of alert child who can ask you one hundred questions between the time school started and the snack period. Her mother had been divorced because she was pregnant with another man's child and was still living with that man three years later. As I thought back about this little six-year-old girl, who had once walked the two miles to school because she had missed the school bus, I came to think again how she was really missing something at home—love. She craved love and attention so much that it hurt; she would do anything just to be noticed and praised. I thought that if only one person in that Church would offer to let her visit on Saturday or Sunday once or twice a month, it would do them both worlds of good. So I wrote to the clergyman, telling him of my hope for this child. Just a little love for a little girl who needed it desperately was all I asked. Love is always hardest to give, I guess, for to really love is to give selflessly of oneself—and that leaves one very vulnerable. That is the only reason I can find for why there was never any response from that parish to this need.

THE "NEW" CHURCH IS ALIVE

The program in which I participated was ecumenically sponsored and the Volunteers—college students for the most part —paid a $100 registration fee, which went toward room and board, and lived in groups of about ten. This past summer, although most were Roman Catholic or Episcopalian, there was tremendous growth and understanding ecumenically in our group. Our group bull sessions would start at the drop of a hat, and we'd be off, delving into various religious doctrines, creeds, politics, or almost any subject. During our frequent and sometimes heated religious discussions, we came to understand more deeply our own and each other's religious beliefs. Each person respected and loved the others, and this relationship grew beautifully during the summer, until we all began to dread leaving what we had found together in this group. We knew that upon departing, a little part of us would go in ten different directions across the United States, from California to Connecticut, from Wisconsin to Lousiana.

One night we got talking about a subject dear to us—the Eucharist. Our two supervisors, both wonderful and sensitive men, who will enter the Roman Catholic priesthood next year, and the group were talking about transubstantiation and the necessity of being a Roman Catholic in order to receive Holy Communion in the Roman Catholic Church. At one point, one of them pointed out that according to the law of his Church, he would have to turn away a non-Roman from the communion rail, whether he believed in transubstantiation or not. Suddenly the pain of separation was very great and very real. The fact that anyone has the right to deny me the Body and Blood of my Lord, even though the law of one Church says that he must, is really frightening. It was the same Christ who died for both of us, and it is Christ's cross we both bear— then why the separation? Everyone left a little shaken that night because we were so close, and this really hurt—this huge unwanted gulf between Church communions. This is why I look with purest joy at the Ecumenical movement which, I believe, will become the "new" Church. Ecumenical, not static, slow, or institutionalized as some of the Churches of today, but free and *alive,* at work in the world which it loves.

Do you believe that this new Church is alive yet? I know it is, and I can show it to you in groups of young people across the United States, giving up time (and money) to work for their fellowmen in poverty programs, VISTA, the Peace Corps, and other like groups. You can identify this Church partially through the deep love of humanity shown by its members and their Christian service. You can hear its angry, demanding shouts as blacks and whites see each other as persons, not as different races, and fight together for freedom that has been too long in coming. You can hear its joy in the laughter of small children, such as those in Head Start programs, like the ones in Wise County.

Yes, the Church, this "new" Church, is alive, active, human, and very real.

16/ The Invisible Christian

by ROBERT E. GROSSMANN

A large number of Christians have become invisible.

As the current phrase would have it, they have gone underground. This is not the first time that this phenomenon has occurred. Records mention a similar tactic almost two thousand years ago. It may seem more than a little romantic to make fanciful comparisons between a candle-lit vigil in the catacombs and a clandestine worship in a high-rise apartment. But comparisons can be made, and they have to be neither romantic nor fanciful.

Since the term "underground" has the type of damp, dark, secretive connotations that we may find difficult to identify with, I would again prefer to say that a substantial number of Christians have become invisible. The early Christians represented a threat to the status quo of their time; they were repressed and, consequently, they did go underground—into the catacombs to worship. Marshall McLuhan might call them antienvironmentalists. They had a message, a life style that did not fit amiably in the contemporary social structure, in their wraparound environment. Their message of love was misunderstood and rejected. One might say that the environment was visible. Like a visual field it represented a continual, unbroken pattern. All the accepted institutions had a place in the social structure and were compatible with a set hierarchy of values. The Christian message was based upon a different value system, it did not fit into the continuum of the social order. It was then, in a sense, invisible.

To become an institutionalized part of the environment Christianity would have had to submit to the then contemporary moral order. It chose rather to address itself to the force which actually formed the environment—the people. The message of Christ was carried through the medium of human interaction and love.

Gradually, with ample use of hook and crook, the Christian movement spread until it became an acceptable and formative force in the environment. But somewhere the medium was lost in the message. The old, prophetic, antienvironmental role became lost as the concepts and functions of Christianity became more diverse and complex. The result, to make a long history short, is the visible church.

The early visible Church could be described in terms of what Thomas Merton calls the Carolingian suggestion. It is a world view that was rooted in the acceptance of the Church into the social and political structure of the Roman Empire. It is predicated upon the assumption that we are living in the last age of salvation history. A world of innate evil has been redeemed from the Devil by the cross of Christ and is simply accumulating years until the message of salvation has been preached to everyone. Then, of course, the judgment will come. In the meantime, the message of love became the message of peace which was really the establishment of order, or, in other words, Roman Law. Freedom in this context is synonymous with chaos and, thus, must be rigorously restricted. The Empire becomes, provisionally at least, holy; the Emperor who is consecrated to Christ becomes the figure of the eschatological kingdom on earth; war on behalf of the Christian prince and his power becomes a holy war for Christ against the Devil. War becomes a sacred duty.

The Carolingian suggestion, slightly altered by the course of historical events, is still with us. It would not be too difficult to describe the contemporary social situation in much the same terminology as used above. For Empire, insert Government. For Devil, insert Communism. There are plenty of other combinations that can be used. The Carolingian suggestion is really the basic pattern for any vertically-structured social order that reinforces its unity by the presence of a constant nameless threat.

In the modern version, however, the Church is conspicuously absent. The contemporary prince does not claim to receive his authority from the Godhead. In one way or another the justification of authority stems from capital. The shakedown throughout the social order is complete. Heaven and hell are no longer the forces they once were in influencing acceptable forms of behavior. The current behavioral sanctions are much more concrete and immediate—position, image, security, wealth, etc.

The Church, in losing ground as an institution which regulates behavior, now has little function outside of its place as an institution among other institutions in the jungle of modern man's social collectivities. Although no longer a formative force in the environment, the visible Church is still an integral element of it. It is part of the continuum that affirms and is predicated upon a value system that permits gross injustices in large segments of society. Still established upon the primacy of social order, still static and hierarchical, it must essentially always align itself with the status quo.

But then there are those Christians who have become invisible. McLuhan observes that the pattern of visibility is a continuum, a uniformity; the visible Church is in and of the environment. The invisible Church is not, nor can it be, integral to such an environment. Neither is the invisible Church itself predicated upon order nor is it easily inscribed in a continuum.

If the invisible Church can be described as an institution, it is a new definition of that term. There is little that is dogmatic about it, and its orthodoxy is nebulous, in a state of flux, or nonexistent. It lives as a social collectivity devoted to liberative personal and communal love-relationships. Social order may be a by-product; but then again, it may not be.

If little is empirically ascertainable about the movement, age is an exception. The great majority of the invisible Church are young people, mostly students. It is the *Time* Man of the Year generation, the Pepsi generation, the Hippie generation that is turning on to invisibility. Is it youthful anarchism or a more permanent, pervasive irresponsibility? This may be the question of the Establishment. There is irony in the question too, especially in the use of the word "responsibility," because of the consistent failure of the established order in the exercise of responsibility—the ability to respond.

The same principles which probably seem primitive when described in the context of the Roman Empire have formed the foundations of our own political structure. The *Federalist Papers* affirm the view that man's basic motivation is his own self-interest. The ideal government would not only contain such impulses but would be designed so that these impulses could be harnessed for the common good. The structure is designed so that even the most egocentric motives become altruistic upon confronting the sublimating influence of law. In a system of checks and balances an individual is allowed to pursue his own self-interests without regard for other people, and the system will correct the bruises and abrasions suffered by the commonweal. Our generation was reared in the doctrine familiar to all previous generations, that, in a sense, it doesn't really make a difference if you have regard for others or know how to communicate or learn what community is all about. As long as you fit into the previously designed structure, you can satisfy all your social obligations with little or no positive effort.

Correlative to the development of the political order is the development of this nation's economy. There is no doubt that the postwar generation is the most affluent collectivity in the history of man. The Pepsi generation, however, has only directly participated as a consumer in this massive accumulation of resources. Thus, the resources are viewed as givens unrelated to the meaning of toil.

This is a revolutionary development in economic history. While the young are sophisticated in the use of this material achievement and understand its value as a means of shaping the environment, industrial-age ideas about the necessity and value of personal ownership are alien. It is becoming clearer and clearer that the pursuit of happiness is not consonant with economic competition because we are learning that insatiable desires are begetting unlimited resources rather than the limited resources we thought we could conquer a few years ago. The personal accumulation of goods is losing the glitter that it once held for young Horatio Algers.

Integral to the economic explosion is the rapid rate of technological development. Of all the automation that surrounds the youth of today, two forms of media—television and computers—have influenced new styles of perception and have been most significant in the extension and compression of their environment. Through TV and films young people are familiar with realities that their parents could ignore. Signals bouncing against satellites are helping to bring about identification with the global community that was impossible in a previous age. America has always been a land of space; it was this space that reinforced the philosophy of rugged individual-

ism, that allowed one to flex his elbows without hitting someone square in the eye. One didn't have to worry about the
community. But mass media, computers, and the rise of the
megapolis have compressed time and space, provoking an existential concern that was not evident in our forefathers, from
Boone to Babbitt.

These two things—economic independence and the development of mass media and computers—are having the most
profound effect on almost all modes of human participation in
this nation. Whether one terms it revolution or generational
gap, it is a change that seems to be taking place at an exponen-
tial rate. Man is, or can be, free from most of the economic
hang-ups that threatened his existence throughout history. He
has the technical tools to build a new world if he so desires.
But this is a decision he has never had to make before. The
established structure had relieved him of *response-ability* by
making all decisions concerning his social obligations for him.
This is a luxury that man can no longer afford. Too many
wrong decisions have been made by the structure; the contin-
uance of such a system threatens the very essence of his humanity. The young man revolts. He tells society that the system will no longer respond for him. He becomes invisible.

This revolution is a cultural phenomenon that transcends
institutional lines. In the student world the estrangement from
the political structure and the institutional Church is also an
alienation from contemporary forms of education which prepare one to enter the system. The race for the grade is more
meaningless and twice as absurd as the economic struggle to
accumulate resources.

Thus, the invisible Christian will probably find that his invisibility is pervading the other arenas of his environment. If
ecclesiastical lines of authority are crumbling, so are authoritarian vertical structures in the secular institutions.

In the massive cataclysm brought about by such a reevaluation of institutions, a cultural background of Christianity is not enough for one to retain allegiance to it as a way of life. Where the Church persists in remaining aloof and insensitive to the needs of the college student, it is ignored or, at best, given the most superficial type of attention by the student himself.

Although the failures of the Church on campus far outweigh its successes, there are a few promising developments. First of all, there is a recognizable need and desire in young people to extend their meaning beyond themselves. This desire was first articulated in the civil rights demonstrations and in the success of organizations such as the Peace Corps and VISTA.

Bonhoeffer's description of Christ as the man for others is making sense to a world come of age. As is evidenced by the Hippie movement there is a strong desire to be for others, to construct new types of community in which an atmosphere of trust and love can be established.

There are a number of prophets of the young invisible Church: the new Beatles, e.e. cummings, and Simon and Garfunkel are a few, and more are emerging. A few rounds with the Beatles' *Sgt. Pepper's Lonely Hearts Club Band* can provide a clearer impression of the frustrations and the needs of young people than can volumes of sociological statistics.

Still, it is apparent that the Church is losing its grasp on the great majority of contemporary youth. It is not adjusting itself quickly enough to the new styles of perception that are becoming increasingly sensitive and sophisticated. For the most of middle-aged America the generational gap is a transitory phenomenon that can be eliminated at age thirty. But, in reality, it appears that the problem of generational incompatibility is likely to get worse long before it can get better. Such gaps begin to open at about age twelve and even occur between young people of only a few years' separation in age. The Church cannot afford to wait for young people to accept it as it is, because that is likely not to happen at all.

My reference to the Christian Church, visible and invisible, has been obviously ecumenical. Ecumenism is a visible-Church word. It can be a game that Churches play. A worship service here, a dialog there—the progressive Church tiptoes through the fields of orthodoxy, seemingly unaware of the reality of human relationships. In some Roman Catholic circles ecumenism is regarded as an entirely different level of activity; to combine it with another goal is like walking and sitting at the same time; it simply can't be done.

The real barriers to ecumenical participation have been culturally rather than ideologically induced. The Virgin Birth has less to do with Church disunity than language or the vague notion that *they* are different than *we* are. Such cultural taboos play a greater role in our behavior than we care to admit. When we try to repress such misgivings and replace them with symbolic rituals, we are taking a step forward, but rarely do we act as a true community in our ecumenical worship service or really listen in a dialog situation.

As was the case with the values of the industrial age, many of the ecumenical hang-ups of the older generation simply do not exist for young people. This is not to say that the wave of the future is mindless conformity or a homogeneous Church. On the contrary, while many young people understand the necessity of solidarity of Christian commitment, it is certain that they will carry out their commitment in diverse ways. There will be differences of opinion, particularly in theological matters, but these differences will be expected and respected rather than merely tolerated.

It is thus impossible to describe specifically the theology of the invisible Church. It has many theologies, all centered around the commandment to love one another. While we live in a society that is becoming increasingly sophisticated in its description of human behavior, ironically we are becoming more and more estranged from the traditional patterns of human communication. While our potential ability to form our environment is greater than it has ever been in human history, we feel that the environment is the hostile master that dictates our pattern of life.

The secular city and the multiversity have created some freedoms and life styles that were not possible in a rural society, but they have succeeded by virtue of their massiveness and complexity in intimidating large portions of our society. People have built walls to protect themselves from the daily risk that compression holds for one's perception of himself, his identity, his security. When enough bricks are piled one on top of another, we are startled to find that not only is it difficult to get in, but it is also difficult to get out. Communication breaks down. Man begins to try to find his identity, his meaning, and his security in himself. But it doesn't work. People need other people.

One of the most active searches in the invisible Church is for viable forms of community. Often this search is centered in forms of worship. The worship or liturgy becomes the symbol of the solidarity of Christian commitment and of the solidarity and love of that community. Because the service is itself a symbolic act, the symbols it uses must speak to the community in a sign and language that the people understand.

Young people understand the metaphors of folk-rock, the penetrating rhythms of jazz, the familiar plasticity of pop art, and the enveloping messages of the film media. All of these expressions are being used to communicate the old and new truths of the gospel. But they mean little if they cannot find a basis in personal experience. The liturgy is not meant to form the community but, rather, to be an expression of that community. Where such experimentation does not enjoy a permissive atmosphere, it is sometimes driven "underground," into the private sector. It is important to note that these efforts to form community are not in themselves the definition of "underground." It is only when the forms are rejected or repudiated by the Establishment that the activities become clandestine.

The mass media have contributed both to the growth and to the mistrust of such activities. A widening gulf is separating the visible and invisible Church. As the established Church sees its dignity and integrity threatened by experimentation, it has a tendency to clamp down even harder, causing frustration and a further barrier to productive conversation within the Church.

Although the invisible Christians are often sharply critical of practices within the visible Church, in a majority of cases they do not wish to sever ties with it. They believe in the people of God as a formative force in history and are hopeful that their commitment can be exercised within the context of the greater body of professing Christians. However, it is becoming increasingly difficult to do this. Even in situations in which the Establishment does not exercise punitive restrictions but rather chooses to ignore or fails to respond to the active forces within it, the frustrations rise.

An important aspect to take into consideration is the usual difference in the world views of the two groups. The visible Church is generally concerned with history through a rearview mirror. It finds justification and reinforcement in tradition. It is an institution, with dignity and integrity, that is based in history. It often looks to the past for answers to the present and the future.

The invisible Church, on the other hand, also believes in history, but it is based in the formation of history. Its world view is eschatological rather than apocalyptic. It does not reject history by this posture; rather, it affirms it as a dynamic expression of the progress of man. Its style of perception is also different. It evaluates social problems in secular terms and is more likely to look to emerging trends for answers to present and future problems.

The Church Establishment is sometimes disturbed by the lack of patience among their more active elements. Sometimes the formal channels of protocol are not utilized nor the traditional diplomatic maneuvering exercised. The impatience is caused by the growing realization that time is not something that catches up with you eventually. The temporal and spatial compression mentioned previously obligates us to make the best possible use of the here and now. The respected formal systems of communication are in many cases archaic to present needs and will fall into disuse by those who feel the urgency of their existential situation.

Riddle: Q. When is a Christian most invisible?
        A. When he is witnessing to his Christian commitment.

The Christian is the man for others. In an effort to be *response-able* he may express his concern through action in the traditional channels. Or he may find it necessary to resort to more radical types of activity. There is a significant invisible Church participation in the myriad movements of the New Left. While it recently has been focalized in the Peace movement, it has also manifested itself in the Black Power movement, radical educational reform, the organization of farm laborers, poverty work, tutorials, community organizing, and many other attempts to meet social needs.

Another significant, yet still emerging, development is the utilization of the findings of behavioral sciences to develop sensitivity and interaction in small communities of people. The use of techniques that are being designed could conceivably have quite an effect on many different styles of programming.

Some of these activities are being carried out in Church-related organizations, but those which prove to be archaic or irrelevant are unhesitatingly ignored in favor of secular channels which may prove more effective. In many other instances the Church is simply not equipped, nor should it be, to provide formal channels of action. In any case, Christian presence is being exerted in a prophetic, reforming stance by those who cannot find acceptable values in the status quo.

In view of this, it is apparent that the Church is confronted with an identity crisis. It can continue its present role of sporadic but inconsistent social involvement. It can continue essentially to align itself with the status quo and the primacy of order. It can base its integrity in the history of the rearview mirror.

Or it can become invisible.

Actually, the alternatives are misleading. For a large number of people the above statements will appear to be somewhat radical. But for a significant number they will be conservative and unduly optimistic. The second group may be smaller—but it is growing daily. It is made up of the people who have been untouched by the Church or have been crushed by it. The Church has not spoken to them, and they are ignoring it. The Church is simply irrelevant. Therefore, there is really a third alternative.

The Church will die.

In the traditional *Hamlet* play, Rosencrantz and Guildenstern are portrayed as somewhat insidious tools of the king, using their friendship to betray the melancholy prince. But in a recent popular British drama, *Rosencrantz and Guildenstern Are Dead,* R and G are presented as two likeable, well-meaning friends who are trapped by their own inability to make a decision. They exert no real presence in the confusing melee of the royal court nor are they able to influence or understand the erratic behavior of Hamlet. R and G do not topple at the end of the play in the traditional bloodbath; rather, it is simply announced that Rosencrantz and Guildenstern are dead. It then becomes clear that R and G are dead because they did not exert a presence, they did not make a decision which really influenced history. There is more than one way to die. Alternatives one and three are painfully similar.

We are at the dawn of a new age if we want to be. But this will necessitate a radical redefinition of all that makes up the social structure. The Church should, by its nature, be a mechanism for change; it isn't presently, but if it chose to lift itself from the tradition and formality that bind it, it would probably be able to make the transition with fewer bruises than other institutions.

There is more to the urgency of this message than simply the internal concerns of the Church, however. There are quite a lot of people who would view the demise of the Church with equanimity, and then try to build anew on the basis of their own personal beliefs. What is really at stake is the freedom of all mankind. Unless the Church resumes its prophetic role, the present structures could collapse with nothing to replace them, or the structures could reinforce themselves by vigorously restricting the freedom of man in the name of order.

A continuing problem that is constantly distorting and delaying the decisions of the Church is the misconception that it plays a major role in defining life patterns. Theology is rarely an explication of the *a priori* truths which order life, but is, when good, an elucidation of present or past phenomena in the light of man's relationship to God and fellow man. Situation ethics was not described to Joseph Fletcher in a vision; rather, it was his analysis of an ethic that was and is already being accepted by a significant number of people. Similarly, it is common knowledge that whatever the Vatican decides in regard to birth control for Catholics, it will have little effect in most countries where contraceptives and drugs are in widespread use. No wonder I flinched when I overheard a man comment in a local coffeehouse, "I am now trying to define what a Christian is. . . ." Could he have meant "describe"?

Unless the Church takes seriously the very real threats to her own existence and to the freedom of mankind, it is unlikely that she will make the basic decisions necessary to pull her out of the fateful Rosencrantz-and-Guildenstern syndrome.

The invisible Church is beginning to make its decisions. It is likely that its ranks will increase in the future as people become more dissatisfied with the confusion in the visible sector. If it is not forced to go underground, it could be the salvation of the remnants of Christianity in the twentieth and twenty-first centuries.

17/ A Bishop Views
the Underground Church

by the RT. REV. PAUL MOORE, JR.

A bishop writing about the Underground Church? Is this a contradiction in terms? Surely a bishop is *above* ground, *way* above ground, maybe too far above the ground. A bishop is a symbol of the institutional, visible Church. He cannot hide. He is usually highly visible, stolidly somewhere in the middle. But as a father in God, he is concerned for all his people, indeed for all people. And if he pretends to the apostolic succession, which is usually thought of as linking the present in strong continuity to the past, he also is a link to the future and, therefore, a link to all the glorious diversity of the present, within and without the Holy Catholic Church. In any case, this particular bishop is honored to contribute to this volume and rejoices in the vitality of the Underground Church. I love the sense of freedom coming forth from this scattering of Christians, which reassures me that we are in an age of the Holy Spirit, a holy spirit of freedom. Freedom, like love, lives a life of its own. It is not an abstraction but a thing. It exists, like the Spirit. Freedom "bloweth where it listeth" and touches a man, a moment, a movement. Gives life. Breaks the iron locks of centuries like the snap of a thread. Catches the dead and brings them to life and laughter.

The anatomy of freedom has been belabored, the word

freedom has been prostituted, but no one is fooled, for freedom slips like mercury out of the hands of anyone who presumes to use it for any ulterior purpose. On the other hand, freedom of the spirit often sparkles most brightly in the lives of men whose bodies are tied down. It comes and breaks open their whole lives when they realize they are in physical or mental chains and as they take the first step to break those chains.

The Underground Church has freedom as its hallmark, because, like Paul in his time and Luther in his, the "underground" has become conscious of the slavery of today's world and today's religion. I personally feel bound, and, in a sense, as part of the institution I am one of the binders. My deepest vocation at this point seems to be the loosening of strictures.

No bonds should tie the Church, no walls separate its life from all life. No forms should be so rigid that they stifle the breath of the Body. However, we in the Church are tied with canonical knots, separated by Gothic walls, stifled by seventeenth-century language and medieval thought forms. These do not kill the Spirit; the Spirit never dies. But they prevent its free operation within the Church so that the Spirit, frustrated as it were, leaves the rigid institution and springs up with new life in unlikely places. You can see these shoots springing up in the fringes of the old Church; they are scattered, whimsically, across the world from university to cotton patch. And so we can say that the Holy Spirit is present when the new life is growing, even when no one recognizes in that life the Church. We can say that the old stump of the Church itself has new shoots of life, even when it is embarrassed by them.

This paper will be concerned with examples of this new life, how it can be recognized, and in what way we can be part of it.

I would say the qualities of the Spirit in the new life include not only freedom, but honesty and love. By honesty, I mean the identification of word with action, of life with belief, of feeling with commitment. By love, I mean a passionate concern for every person as a human being of infinite worth, a concern expressed in service to that person as if he were the Lord.

Thus, the mode of articulation of the Spirit, the means of the revealing of the Spirit, is, in our day, through person, through community of persons, and through event. This may seem obvious: From where else could revelation come? Yet, the Church, the university, and even the body politic still seek orthodoxy through abstract statement, through ideology, through doctrine, or through esthetics, a particular view of the nature of beauty. We who call ourselves contemporary Christians see reality in the Christ-figure, the most despised of men; we sense the Spirit present as the bread-breaking breaks barriers or commemorates bodies broken for others. There is no other orthodoxy, we say, but Christ-love freely given, sparkling through the diversities of persons in whom we believe he dwells. The bible is the history of that love; the creed, a pledge of loyalty in that love; the Eucharist, the pattern and the power of that love.

Enough for abstractions. How easy it is to spiel them off even while denying their validity.

Listen first to the sound of the Spirit in the Underground Church outside the Church.

"BUILD NOT BURN" is its slogan.

From its founding statement:

We seek the establishment of a democracy of individual participation governed by two central aims: That the individual share in those social decisions determining the quality and direction of his life; that the society be organized to encourage independence in men and provide the media for their common participation. . . .

From a speech of its president:

Our best concern. . . . *is to make love more possible*. We work to remove from society what threatens and prevents it—the inequity that coordinates with injustice to create plain suffering and to make custom of distrust, poverty, racism, the assembly line universities of this Pepsi generation, the ulcerating drive for affluence.

From a recent statement:

We are fully prepared for service to our country and to democracy. We volunteer to go into Watts to rebuild that neighborhood the way the people of Watts want it to be, and when we say rebuild we mean socially as well as physically. We volunteer to serve in VISTA or the Peace Corps to help them learn, as we have been learning in the slums and Mississippi, how to energize the hungry and desperate and deflated of the world to make the big decisions about their own future and to carry out those decisions.

Our generation is not afraid of service for long years and low pay: we have been working for years in the slums of America at $10 a week to build a movement for democracy there. We are not afraid to risk our lives in Alabama and Mississippi, and some of us have died there. But we will not bomb the people, the women and the children of another country.

I have little firsthand experience of the members of the community whose statements of belief you have just read. But I understand they remain true, in their lives, to these words. Who are they? Are they members of a parish, a new Christian sect, a Franciscan Order? No, they are members of the "notorious" Students for a Democratic Society. I am sure there is cynicism, jealousy, posturing within S.D.S. I am not sure how long S.D.S. will last. I would say, however, that here and there in the small communities of such a group the Underground Church is a reality, *incognito,* dressed in strange secular, even atheistic, costumes, but definitely and clearly present. Whenever two or three are gathered together in the name of love, Christ is present through the Spirit, though no one may call him by name.

This is the point, however, at which to show the need for a consciousness of his presence if a community is to remain a loving place, if a movement is to remain a community of love. I do not believe any organization can constructively grow, certainly no organization can exist in the Spirit, if it separates itself from the rest of mankind and returns anger for anger. And I do not believe that any such organization can long survive.

Some outside reference point, some objective criterion, some incorruptible presence, some transcendent force whose power lies outside the feelings, the frustrations, the normal human reactions of the group, must be present within it, working to continue the criticism, the judgment, the constant reformation of the group. Otherwise, the politics of the power struggle which exists within any organization and the destructive forces brought to bear upon its slender initiative can twist and destroy it. On the other hand, the danger of such an outside reference point is its idolization, its dehumanization. An example of the improper presence of such a standard is the

Communist Party whose ideology did not purify its members, but instead came to destroy their personal growth and power for good.

We search then for such a presence. A presence of power deep enough to deal with demonic forces within and the principalities and powers without, yet a power flexible, sensitive, dynamic. We seek a person-preserving power, not a person-destroying power. We seek no constricting ideology but a spirit which is freeing. We find it in the breaking of bread. We call it the Eucharist. By constant reenactment of the Eucharist, Christian bodies have been able to purify themselves; by constant conscious relationship with the person of Christ, Christian bodies have been reformed again and again. The constant opening up of the Eucharist has allowed the reentry of the Spirit.

First, I should describe what I mean by the eucharistic action. The eucharistic action is the way in which men participate with Christ in the bringing of the kingdom to society and to individuals. The action exists in the universe, goes on within and without the Church. It is another way of describing what happens when the spirit of freedom and love breaks forth. The elements of the action are acted out in *the* Eucharist, in the Church, celebrated for all occasions in any place. But sometimes its power is almost completely hidden when the celebration occurs officially within the conventional Church; at other times, eucharistic action in power occurs outside the Church without anyone knowing it by name. People experience a strange and lovely blessing and cannot account for its source.

The Eucharist contains these themes:

1. You listen to one another, to the Other, with your whole self. 2. You respond with commitment to what is heard and to him who speaks the truth. 3. You give yourself to one another in love and then give yourselves, united, to the high-

est, the deepest, reality you know. You include in this giving, by thought—some call it prayer—the rest of humanity. 4. Despite the imperfections of this process, the Spirit of Christ becomes present and somehow joins with himself all who participate through the bread and wine on the table. 5. The bread is broken-death, the different kinds of death, is faced-suffering, fear, death of self. 6. The meal is taken—we break bread together, we break bodies together, we sweat together, we receive from each other, from the bread and wine, from Christ, the joy of the kingdom.

This eucharistic action can be described in a thousand ways. It can be very private and personal—an old man receives the bread as he lies dying; a bride and groom seal their love with it the morning of a wedding. It can be an action in which the whole world participates—the Requiem of President Kennedy. It can pick up the agony of a moment and show its deepest meaning to be joy: a Eucharist on an ironing board outside the bombed-out Freedom House in McComb, Mississippi. All these were known to be Eucharists. But there are other times and other places when the eucharistic action has broken through without the event being officially a Eucharist, a Mass. These events, happenings, can be called eucharistic without belaboring, in what may well be passé theological categories, whether such and such an occasion *was* or *was not* a Mass, a "valid" Eucharist.

For those readers who were not brought up in a Catholic tradition, let me explain why I even mention the niceties of whether or not such and such is a valid Eucharist or Mass. For at least fifteen hundred years the Church has preserved the Eucharist against historical pressures that have tried to make it become something other than what it is because the Church knows its life is bound to the Eucharist. The immense value of the action experienced by millions for two thousand years is attested by, for instance, the heritage of Christian architecture. Eucharistic theology makes careful definition of meaning; eucharistic liturgy describes the variations of word and action; eucharistic hymnody conveys the feeling-tone of historic interpretations; Catholic polity (Church government) clarifies under what authority the event can take place. All of this historically has been worked out to safeguard the Eucharist for people.

Now, however, with the Eucharist, as with so much else, there is a stirring toward freedom, a wrestling against the preservations of the past which seem no longer to conserve but to bind.

The so-called Underground Church is often the scene of eucharistic action outside the canonical restrictions of the Churches.

Let me give you an example of an exciting event which occurred in the most unexciting context of a Church-sponsored youth weekend. The young people were a random cross section of Washington high-school students, many of them having rejected faith in formal Christianity. I had agreed to go on the weekend on the condition that I could listen to what they believed rather than be asked to tell them what I believed. Since belief is of the feelings, the innermost self, as well as of the mind, we worked out ways in which their belief could be expressed in action and music as well as in conversation.

We role-played a situation involving friendship and love between two boys and a girl and investigated our beliefs about honesty and love. We listened to music and spoke of why we were caught up by it. We danced. We took long walks and had long talks together. A sense of community grew among us as the hours passed, although we were from different backgrounds, races, ages. On the final morning the group, with no clerical assistance, put together the most moving service I have almost ever attended. It began in quietness. A raucous recording burst in: "Bang Bang Oooh She Freaks." Silence again. Readings from Robert Frost's *Fire and Ice*. Silence. Passage from St. Paul . . . "Now we see through a glass darkly, then face to face." Silence. Passage from *A Separate Peace* by John Knowles . . . "All of us, at infinite cost to ourselves, construct these Maginot Lines against the enemy we think we see across the frontier. The enemy who never attacks that way . . . if he attacks at all . . . if he is indeed the enemy. . . ."

Comment from one who had said very little: "I couldn't role-play. I tried but I just couldn't. This meant to me we can't live in false roles and have life mean anything . . . we must be honest. Maybe it's up to us, now that we know what we have learned, 'how the world ends . . . fire or ice' [a quote from Robert Frost]."

Silence, followed by another comment:
"It's the loneliness.
"We don't want to be lonely alone.
"That's why we talk about it so much."

Silence. A rather distant-sounding voice from another:

God, are you listening? Who is listening? I hurt someone, God. Now I hurt, because I realize how much I love him. . . . For such a long time I hated him for not loving me, even after what I had done. We both have suffered pain, God. We both have hated and loved, at different times, of course. *Love, Hate, Pain:* Help us, Lord, to put these three things together. Love and hate are one and the same; pain is the process of love and hate. Help us God to put our love and hate together. I am ready to try, Lord. I am ready to give my all.

The listening and the responding concluded. Now was the time of giving.

A simple ballet. Two stand apart, with heads against the wall, holding brass collection plates. They dance past each other. And again. Finally, they dance toward each other and meet and embrace. This is their offering as they pass the plates symbolically around the room. Music—the Beatles' "We can work it out."

Silence, interspersed by thoughts of others, prayers for others. I remember one especially; I pray for his parents in their loneliness for him.

Finally, we sit in a circle, break bread, and toast, one by one, in great joy our happening. In the background I could hear *Lord of the Dance*.

LORD OF THE DANCE*

I danced in the darkness and the world was begun,
And I danced in the moon and the stars and the sun.
I came down from heaven and I danced on the earth,
In Bethlehem I had my birth.

Chorus: Dance then, wherever you may be,
I am the Lord of the Dance, said he,
And I'll lead you all wherever you may be,
I will lead you all in the dance, said he.

I danced into Galilee and danced by the sea
And men dropped their nets and came dancing after me
I danced for the cripples, for the sinners and the sad
They joined in the dance and their hearts were glad.

* Sidney Carter, "Lord of the Dance" in *Risk* Vol. II, 3 (1966), p. 31, "New Hymns for a New Day," World Council of Churches, Geneva, Switzerland.

I danced on the Sabbath and I danced for the priest
I danced in the temple and I called them to the feast
I danced for the scribe and for the Pharisee
But they would not dance and follow me.

They thought when they killed me that the dancing was done
But I am the dance and the dance goes on
I danced down the alleys and the streets of Hell
The dead rejoiced and they danced as well.

I danced back to earth and into Galilee
My friends danced again and came dancing after me
I dance on in heaven and the trumpets shall ring
Calling us to dance at the courts of the King.

It is hard to convey the immense feeling of excitement which exploded there and to comprehend the spirit which continued for many months among us. And, I am sure, even in many a less-structured situation, the eucharistic spirit has been present.

There are even deeper mysteries in the Eucharist than those we have mentioned. These are the mysteries which we Christians call the Incarnation and the Resurrection. It is heartbreaking that these very words are enough to turn young people away, for the words, used so glibly by the Church, echo impossible Sunday-School classes or neurotic voices screaming over the radio on a Sunday morning.

Incarnation is enfleshment, the presence of God in the flesh, the blood, the sweat, and the love of humanity. When the Freedom movement was at its height and strangers were caught up together in its power, many sensed another presence in the hot Church basements of Mississippi and on the long, dusty road in Alabama. The presence of danger, the presence of blood, the presence of deep affection among strangers, which touched the innermost responses of love, each was the presence of Christ, *incognito*. These persons, like the men on the road to Emmaus, felt his presence in the flesh of their brother, without knowing who he was, without recognizing him whom we call Christ. On the other hand, there are churchmen practicing an emaciated piety who have never known their Lord's presence in their fellowmen. We call this presence the Incarnation, for it first was shown forth in the person of Jesus himself.

The bread and wine are a symbol of this; the best of the spirit abroad at Christmas is the joy of it. This reality explains why sometimes one feels like genuflecting before the body of a poor man suffering.

The Resurrection describes the new birth and joy which comes forth after a period of pain. God knows, the younger generation experiences the pain of separation, of what is called "alienation." Some of them know, as well, the intensity of joy which breaks into their lives when this pain is relieved by love, whether it be the love of another person or the love of a new community, like the best of the Hippie community. They also know that the joy is not stable, that it ebbs and flows, that its ebbing is a new suffering and its flooding again a higher joy. They have participated in the pulsating rhythm of Christian life.

This, too, is symbolized by the Eucharist. For in it we die to each other, and in it, somehow, we join ourselves to the mighty primeval wresting from night of the dead body of Jesus Christ.

I could go on rambling, recounting anecdotes, themes, principles of life which are caught up in the Eucharist, for it is a symbol, an action catching all of Christian life, indeed all of any kind of life.

This takes us another step, to a bold statement made by others but not yet stated unequivocally and officially by the Church because its enormous implications may take many a day, perhaps generations, to work through. I am not sure it can be truthfully and fully said, and yet the tendency of the freeing spirit is pushing us to that logical conclusion, namely, that the Church is coterminous with humanity itself, that no rigid line can be drawn between Christians and others.

If this be true, and in some sense the most conservative theologian would agree to it by such a statement as "Jesus died for all men, not just for Christians"; if this be true, the role of the Church is altered and brought back to what Jesus himself seemed to describe. Jesus exalted the kingdom of God, not the institutional Church. He found the kingdom outside the Jewish Church as well as within it. His deepest anger was reserved for those who pretended to religion but were unloving. He saw his disciples as kingdom-recognizers and kingdom-bringers, as those who, because they were close to him, could recognize his kingdom, as those who, because they took part in the Eucharist, could sense his presence, the eucharistic presence, wherever they found it. The early Christians' joy in this Eucharist drew others into their fellowship, and all were welcome who changed their way of life according to the spirit of the kingdom.

The early Christian Church was an Underground Church, rebelling against Judaism, yet catching up the best in Judaism, living in a new spirit of freedom and love, searching for form. During the first three hundred years there was no Creed, no ordered ministry, no New Testament. The uniting and empowering action was the Eucharist.

This gives a clue to the vocation of the present Underground Church. These new Christians are rebelling against the old forms which, in so many cases, are no longer appropriate for the spirit of freedom and love. They seek to include—and, indeed, feel themselves brothers to—those who do not acknowledge themselves Christian, the many who are so infected with the spirit of love and freedom that they are not drawn to conventional Churches where the love is at best hidden and the freedom is at most interior The Underground Christian lives, at his best, in a eucharistic spirit, acting as a leaven within those secular organizations which seek the goals of the kingdom, seeking to maintain that spirit against the normal corruptions of human societies.

The Eucharist is the symbol and power of unity for the Underground Church. But because of the depth of unity of these Underground Christians, the unity of the rest of the Church is threatened by their existence. In seeking their community with Christians of other denominations and with like-minded loving persons outside the institutional Church, they weaken their ties with those within the Church who do not share their convictions. It has been stated many times that a future great schism may occur in the Church, across denominational lines, between those (characterized by the "underground") who share the passionate and radical concern for their fellowman and those who cling to a religion which is content with the so-called spiritual side of the gospel, between those who feel the Church must be involved in shaping society or be left to die at the roadside of history and those who would be content to remain on the sidelines in peace.

Let no one underestimate the depth of this tension on every side. I used to have lunch about once a month with a rabbi, a Presbyterian minister, a Methodist minister, and a Catholic priest. Each one of us had exactly the same problems with the lay leadership of our respective congregations. A much deeper tie existed between us clergy than between us and the lay leadership; we shared far more belief between ourselves than we did with those members of our congregations who knew and loved a pietistic Church.

Many of us are concerned by the inverse ratio between Church attendance and the desire for social change among Church members. If social change is the principal way in which men's lives can be made better on any substantial scale, we must admit that attendance at Church is inclined to lessen realistic concern for one's fellow and that those who wish to keep the status quo are also those who are drawn to the conventional Church. It may seem presumptuous to label one kind of Church life "more Christian" than another, but at the risk of such presumption I would say that we must take a long hard look at conventional Church life and ask whether or not it *is* Christianity. If it is not, should Church officials be concerned about the dropping away of conservative Church members when they are really dropping away from the Church's expression of love? This is the difficult question. It would wreck the institution. It is easy for one to posture as a brave prophetic voice for social change and snarl at the "hypocrites" who do not agree. But in that course there is a demonic temptation perhaps even more sinister than old-fashioned institutionalism. From the moment such a stand is taken, one has lost a sense of compassion for another human being, he has exalted himself as judge, and he has put another wound in the Body of Christ. On the other hand, the integrity of the Church cannot be compromised to please those who find it uncomfortable.

What way is left, then, to deal with the growing tension? How can you minister to the "underground" and to the Establishment? How can one preach a gospel which can be heard in an eighteenth-century rural church, a swinging ghetto church, a sophisticated Georgetown church? Perhaps the task is impossible, and yet this is the vocation of a bishop. To do this and also to speak forth in such a way as to be heard by the world: this is our task. And further, the strength of the total institution gives power to the ministry of love, to the ministry to the poor.

Underground Christians: Do not, then, be too quick to judge those who sometimes seem to be slow in leading the Church in a forward way. Do not hesitate to make loud noises at them, for such loud noises are useful to them, but do not impugn their integrity. And by the same token, see as part of your own job a compassionate understanding for those who have not yet been touched by the spirit of freedom.

The Christian has been always called to a ministry of reconciliation. To be the man in the middle is to follow our Lord. And today there are few of us who do not in some way share in this ministry of the man in the middle. For today it is hard to be so far to the left that no one thinks you an Uncle Tom or its equivalent. And I trust that no Christian is so far to the right that no one thinks him a little soft on Communism. The poles today are far apart. For this reason, sometimes it is necessary to make a human chain across the chasm, from right to left, so that some communication can continue. Here is a spot for the Underground Christians—to act as communicators across the great barriers of American society, to be revolutionaries so free that they can love and speak with those against whom they revolt.

Underground Christians have a special opportunity, for they move freely from Church to Church, drawn to those places where new life is springing up. They are somehow minstrels, wandering lovers at home with Jews, "pagans," Protestants, Catholics, wherever such men and women are part of the kingdom.

For such a free flowing brotherhood, one constant is necessary: there must be one continuing channel of communication with the Holy Catholic Church, the communion of Saints of the ages. Let this channel be the Eucharist which can play the central unifier and be the pattern and the power of this kingdom today, as once it was when the Church was young.

Let me rejoice once more in the Underground Church. To its members belongs the sacred spirit of the future. But in their enthusiasm, in their impatience, they must remain open to those who still labor under institutional responsibilities. They must be sensitive to the diversity of vocation which each is given.

May all of us live and grow within the eucharistic kingdom.

18/ Imitatio Christi

by MALCOLM BOYD

I see no "beautiful tomorrow." However, neither do I see a necessarily "ugly tomorrow." I question what is the meaning of "tomorrow." I find "progress" is subject to vastly different interpretations and is certainly laced by unchanging moral ambiguities. "Power" must constantly be challenged in ways which are precise and specific, can shatter friendships, and will cost so much pain, so many dollars, and so much in blood. One "revolution" ushers in another, or, at least, calls for one even across decades or centuries.

I find hope in today, not tomorrow. We are responsible for *now*. We are called to live, witness, love, and be servants *now*. *Now* is the moment of my expectation and hope. *Now* is the road, the desert, the city, the happening, even "Jerusalem." If I look forward to "Jerusalem" very carefully, making elaborate plans for it, I may never realize its reality and only feel a certain numbness concerning a sensitivity which perished or a death which somehow did not get died.

"Freedom *now!*" says a young black nationalist in a Newark slum, and so does his brother, a middle-aged white pastor in a middle-class suburban parish, who feels trapped amid the externals of cultic symbolism, organizational activism, and small talk.

The author gratefully acknowledges the kindness of *Jubilee* for permission to use material which first appeared in its pages.

How can one *put* his life, if he wishes to give it, with integrity, for social justice? Answers must depend upon basic hypotheses within men's lives. For example, if one is speaking from the standpoint of *imitatio Christi* as such a hypothesis, one is, it seems to me, required to render "social justice" as nonabsolute and "the kingdom of God" (by whatever name) as absolute. In other words, *for* what is one giving his life if he predicates the gift on the basis of *imitatio Christi?* "Social justice," by itself, may issue in such a poignant, yet simplistic, description as the "beautiful tomorrow." In what structures is this gift of one's life to be formalized? In what place? Doing what? The answer will depend largely on one's definition of *imitatio Christi* and, therefore, of Jesus Christ. There will be neither "good" nor "bad" structures; all will have possibilities.

However, more needs to be said to both the young black nationalist who feels trapped in the structure of a Newark ghetto and the middle-aged white pastor who feels hopeless within the structure of a church, that is, a building in the middle of a block as well as a dot on a map in an office which is a headquarters for a "diocese" or a Church "district." Neither man can see clearly, in this moment, where to put, or give, his life. In fact, neither one believes much of a choice is open to him. Is life simply going on, hoeing the row, without sensible or meaningful alternatives? In either the case of the man in the Newark slum or the middle-class white parish —assuming that *imitatio Christi* possesses meaning as a dynamic—a person is confronted by "the kingdom of God": *Has* it come? *Is* it here? Or *isn't* it? One experiences a quite different condition of hope when he believes "the kingdom of God" is an existing reality, instead of depending upon oneself for its possible, and future, existence. In some highly paradoxical ways, the young black nationalist may possibly be affording a clearer picture of *imitatio Christi* than his white pastor brother who may be talking about it professionally while feeling remoter from it as a dynamic reality.

The archaisms of the term "the kingdom of God" get in the way for both the man in Newark and the man in the parish. Neither can easily relate to "kingdom" and, for each, "God" is becoming more and more difficult as a word and concept. Yet there is a radical difference between a ground of being and no ground.

The Underground Church, as a movement, is aware of the irony that "orthodoxy" may largely have passed from Establishment "defenders of the faith" to protesters against the corruptions contained in "American Christianity." Here, one must come to terms with what has been called secular spirituality. I have been asked: "Is not one of the dangers of the words 'secular spirituality' bound up in the fact that American civilization and American Christianity have become one piece of plywood which is now curvaceously warped? And if you agree to this warping, would you feel that our civil and spiritual renewal must come from some other continent or peoples? Where is the civil civilization of the future?"

Secular spirituality stands with the "orthodoxy" of protest *against* the very perversions contained within the practice of a Christianity which goes hand-in-hand with "nigger" and "napalm." The Establishment Church seems to be a very chaplain of the status quo, socially and economically, standing over against the dispossessed and suffering victims of this same status quo. It does not seem to want its position as a major real-estate operator to be upset by prophetic disturbance.

Secular spirituality is simply spirituality expressed in modern form and, at the same time, represents an attempt to preserve the content of the gospel as over against cultural interpretations of it which have come under the captivity of nationalism, colonialism, Puritanism, and Fundamentalism.

The *now* quality of secular spirituality is based, first, on the content of the gospel (the relation of God to man in the person of Jesus Christ) and, second, on contemporary expression and form. This can be misleading if one only looks at it superficially and sees, on the surface, a supposed accommodation to culture. Actually, here is a sharp cutting-edge set against the accommodation marked by the "orthodoxy" of the "defenders of the faith" representing the Establishment Church which has treated ecumenism bureaucratically and defensively from behind high denominational walls and has allied "the Church" with power structures in tight class castes.

I think that "our civil and spiritual renewal" must probably come from within rather than from without; in other words, not so much "from some other continent or peoples" as from the development of *imitatio Christi* within ourselves. The Underground Church seems to be a movement responding in this way to this crisis; the emergence of a secular spirituality is linked to it. And this does not so much mean creating a new prose and music for "worship"; it calls, first, for an awareness of life as holy and of God as being in the midst of it.

Profanity, then, is more likely to be found in "religious" separatism, legalism, or self-righteousness than in vernacular verbal expressions, breaking of churchly laws, or a sacramental understanding of the celebration of life. The "civil and spiritual renewal" of a people who are racist must come from within the fabric of that people; so too in the case of a people who develop militarily (and psychologically) toward the potential of genocide. The gospel does not need to go underground to maintain its integrity; but a people may need to go underground to respond in integrity to the gospel, and, in that response, discover the community from which servanthood emerges in secular, worldly forms.

This could be called "withdrawal"; but it might be the very

withdrawal of involvement. It means ceasing to use certain patterns and forms in favor of others and, therefore, involves a basic change in attitude concerning the meanings underlying the patterns and forms.

I recall, for example, an incident which shook my attitudes and actually changed some basic forms in my own life as a Christian. I was spending a period of time, during the summer of 1965, in rural Mississippi and Alabama, working with the Student Nonviolent Coordinating Committee. I was living, working, and traveling with four other men, all of whom were black. At the outset, one of them told me, "You're white and we can't live this intimately and for this amount of time with a white. So you'll have to be a nigger like we are." This had precise meanings. The four, all veterans of the movement, had spent time in jails for "civil rights offenses" (one had been sentenced to thirty days on a chain gang). To be "nigger" meant that we shared, alike, the rural shacks in which a place could be found to sleep; one meal a day, from an impoverished black family, if we were lucky; implicit white contempt and overt rejection (denial of use of bathroom facilities at a service station or the use of a water fountain in a public place —these incidents, *after* the United States Government's passing of "civil rights" legislation); police and civilian harassment and psychological brutality; and threats of death. (This was a year marked by continuing murders of civil rights workers.)

I remember the first Sunday morning when the five of us were initially together; we were in a small town in Mississippi. Where would I go to church? To receive the eucharistic sacrament in my own denomination would have meant separating myself from my brothers. Would I have "found" Jesus in the consecrated bread and wine inside a segregated white-church building closed to my black brothers (indeed, one in which I would probably have had to disguise my own identity)? Or was Jesus "with us" in our Sunday meal? It is a complex question to which there are not simple answers. This experience did much actually to change my basic attitudes about the Church and the sacraments; I departed, at the end of the summer, with a sense of God's freedom from man's definitions and controls.

For several years, I served as a white in a "Negro church," assisting two different black priests. The charade of "Negro church" was perpetuated, despite pronouncements by Church leaders and public churchly resolutions, because middle-class whites chose not to live near middle-class Negroes and, therefore, not to worship God with them. Yet I found that middle-class Negroes have the same sex habits as middle-class whites, read the same magazines (with the exception of *Ebony*), and mix a Martini in the same way. What were we all *doing* Sunday mornings at eleven in our separated churches in our segregated neighborhoods? Such a question forces one to look deeper into the very meaning of "the Church," "spirituality," and "worship."

The ghetto of Sunday morning at eleven, quite aside from color barriers, becomes even demonic when one has realized, while participating in "worship," that napalm was at that very hour being dropped by Americans on Vietnamese men, women, and children, and their land. One wanted to run screaming or shouting outside that church building, for the "worship"—in its callous indifference to life and total disinterest in napalm *or* the Vietnamese—had become a deadening, frightening, antiseptic, cellophaned, even blasphemous event *outside of life*. (One wondered, in that moment, was God somehow more *outside* that building than in it?)

In August, 1967, I attended, with some forty other Americans, a conference in Bratislava, Czechoslovakia, with nearly forty Vietnamese. They represented the National Liberation Front of South Vietnam (NLF) and the Democratic Republic of North Vietnam (DRV). So, to most Americans, they would be "Communists" and "Vietcong," as, to most Vietnamese, we would be "American imperialists." Yet we talked, laughed, cried, broke bread together, and were *a community*.

I felt very strongly the presence of the Underground Church in the sessions; whatever spirituality emerged there was, assuredly, "secular."

Certainly, the Church—encompassing all the movements within it as well as its ruling elites—will continue to exist as an institution. It will live in the tension generated by the stirrings of the prophetic vis-à-vis the solidity of the Establishment, by personal expressions of spirituality vis-à-vis the calling of moral involvement in contemporary issues, and by the dictates of individual conscience vis-à-vis the demands of obedience to corporate authority.

So, in a sense, the future of the Church will consist of merely new chapters on old themes. The metaphysical dimension of life will not shrivel up and die; "God" (or ". . .") by whatever name, will continue to be killed, buried, resurrected, and, Job-like, furiously dealt with; the young will go on dreaming their dreams while the old perceive great visions, and vice versa.

Church history is, essentially, a story of human beings, with a tendency to be either at their best or worst. Looking ahead (but how absurd: it is as if one were predicting San Francisco's slipping beneath the waters of the bay to join Atlantis, a renaissance of royalty in Spain, or Jacqueline Kennedy's marriage), I see what must now appear (but will not *then*) as cataclysmic changes in the Church as within the total society.

Population explosion. Nuclear destruction or a viable "United Nations." Racial war or accommodation. Distribution of goods or poverty revolutions, or both. Open societies or fascist concentration camps, or both. Well, then. Against such social alternatives, the Church will either have the faithfulness and courage to will its death, so that it may experience resurrection, or will resist that dying and newness to which the underground is committed. What do I think will happen?

"The Church" will be seen less and less as a building, on a corner, to be visited to confess masturbation and adultery and to indulge in a period of "magic." Smaller Christian communities will replace larger ones; clergy will be employed in "the world," and the lay-clerical dichotomy will be relaxed—so there will be clerical functions with only distant memories of a priestly mystique; cult will continue, but God alone knows precisely how; "prayer," as we have known it, will be unheard-of, for the other figure in prayer is God, who is, absurdly and actually, being redefined; the patently ridiculous, assumed contradiction between mysticism and pragmatism will vanish; morality will not be seen as a neat category; Newman Clubs, Canterbury Clubs, Wesley Foundations, Westminster centers, and other denominational campus ghettos will have slipped beneath a convenient bay; Vatican XVIII will be urgently awaited; some will be tentatively suggesting clerical celibacy as a unique idea for institutional purification; the Buddhist-Christian dialogue will be the subject of a major piece in the Sunday *Times;* a black Pope will take the unprecedented step of naming a white Cardinal (an ex-Anglican, at that); and there will be furious, underground rumblings concerning the need for an absolute revolution in the Church in order to avoid its demise within a decade.

Meanwhile, however, the arena in which we find ourselves is *now*. Our basic task is neither to study history nor predict the future, but to live responsibly so that there may be a history to chronicle and a future in which other men and women may have the opportunity to live. For many, the Underground Church is seen as a present and necessary way of experiencing Jesus Christ in community and, therefore, is the basis of social possibilities for human servanthood. Increasingly, Underground Churches, like catacombs, will be found as communities. It is understood that these do not comprise a "new" Church but a locus for community, worship, and service. Action of Church unity will continue to be matched by radical (not liberal) participation in social concerns. *Imitatio Christi* will come to mean, more and more, the development of a Christian secular, rather than a "religious," style of life.